The Atlas of
WORLD
RELIGIONS

The Atlas of
WORLD

This edition first published in 2005 by
Franklin Watts
96 Leonard Street,
London EC2A 4XD

Franklin Watts Australia
45-51 Huntley Street,
Alexandria, NSW 2015

ISBN 0 7496 5920 3

The Atlas of World Religions was created and produced by
McRae Books Srl, Borgo Santa Croce, 8 – Florence (Italy)
info@mcraebooks.com

Series editor Anne McRae
Illustrations Paola Ravaglia, Studio Stalio (Alessandro Cantucci,
Fabiano Fabbrucci, Andrea Morandi, Ivan Stalio), Lorenzo Cecchi,
Leonardo Meschini, Franco Autuori, Ferruccio Cucchiarini, Gian Paolo Faleschini

Picture research: Loredana Agosta
Graphic Design Marco Nardi
Editing Loredana Agosta
Layout and cutouts Laura Ottina, Adriano Nardi, Filippo Delle Monache

A CIP catalogue record for this book is available from the British Library

Colour separations Litocolor, Florence

Printed in Singapore

THE ATLAS OF
WORLD RELIGIONS

Anita Ganeri

W
FRANKLIN WATTS
LONDON • SYDNEY

Contents

Note – This book shows dates as related to the conventional beginning of our era, or the year 0, understood as the year of Christ's birth. All events dating before this year are listed as BCE, or Before Current Era (eg. 928 BCE). Events dating after the year 0 are defined as CE, or Current Era (eg. 24 CE), wherever confusion might arise.

Left: prehistoric people painted animals and hunting scenes on cave walls. The paintings may have been drawn as part of a religious ritual to ensure better hunting.

Right: this statue dates back to about 30,000 BCE and may be a figure of an early goddess.

Early religion

Ancient people tried to explain the world around them as the work of the gods. They believed that the gods controlled everything in nature and their daily lives. They prayed and made offerings to the gods for the gifts of sun and rain which allowed the plants to grow so that people could survive. From these early prayers and offerings, the idea of organized religion grew, with people sharing their rituals and religious beliefs.

Laws to live by

Religion provides many followers with a code for life, a set of rules or laws to live by. These rules or laws are intended to help followers live a better life on Earth.

Left: the Jews use the Torah, a holy book, as a guide for their lives.

Creation of the world

Many religions explain the creation of the world and everything in it as the work of God, the gods or a supreme being. These beliefs are expressed in creation myths which not only try to explain more about how the world was created but also why it came to be.

Right: mythology and storytelling play an important part in many of the world's religions. In Australia, a didgeridoo player traditionally accompanies an Aborigine storyteller.

Below: this 16th-century illustration is a symbolic representation of a supreme being or creator.

Good and evil

Many religions try to explain the nature and presence of good and evil in the world as the work of a good, loving God and a wicked, sinful Devil. But one of the hardest questions for religions to answer is why, if God is good, there is so much suffering in the world. Many people say that suffering happens when people turn away from God or they explain suffering as God's punishment for sin.

Right: in the Middle Ages, people believed that if they led wicked lives, they might be caught and eaten by the Devil.

Introduction

This book traces the history and spread of the world's great religions, from the ancient beliefs of the past to the living faiths of today. There are many different religions around the world, each with its own set of beliefs and ways of worshipping. Some religions are followed by millions of people. Others are locally-held beliefs. Whether large or small, most religions share a common purpose. They try to explain the great mysteries of life, such as how the world was created and why, how a person should live his or her life on Earth, what happens when a person dies and why there is suffering in the world. Some religions, such as Judaism, Christianity and Islam, have just one God. They are called monotheistic religions (the word monotheism means 'believing in one God'). Other religions, including some of those practised in Africa and Asia, are polytheistic ('believing in many gods'). While most religions do have gods or spirits, not all of them have a supreme being or group of gods. Many are more like spiritual guidelines or ways of life to help followers lead happy and rewarding lives.

Above: the Sikh emblem, called the nishan sahib, *consists of a steel ring which represents God's unity, and a two-edged sword symbolizing justice and truth. The two crossed, curved swords around the outside signify the spiritual power of God.*

Below: statue of Gopoka, one of the first disciples of the Buddha.

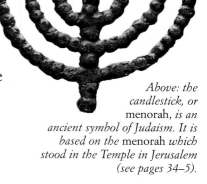

Above: the candlestick, or menorah, is an ancient symbol of Judaism. It is based on the menorah which stood in the Temple in Jerusalem (see pages 34–5).

Above: this statue shows the Hindu god Shiva in the form of the Lord of Ganas, a dwarf. Hindus worship many different gods and goddesses who represent aspects of a supreme being, called Brahman or God.

Many paths

Some people believe that they have the power within themselves to make sense of life and to improve the world for everyone, without needing to rely on God. Buddhists follow the Buddha's teachings in their lives but do not worship him as a god. They honour him as a very special human being who showed them a way to live in order to achieve happiness and peace.

Right: in Christianity, a cross is a symbol of Jesus. This is a very early cross from Italy.

Right: a 7th century Islamic coin from Damascus in Syria. The Arabic inscription reads, 'There is no God but God alone.'

Death and the afterlife

Many people believe in the afterlife, or life after death. They believe that the soul, or the spirit of a person, continues to live after the body dies. Some religions have their own sets of rules and rituals for death. When a person dies, many take special care of the body and prepare a special burial place. In many ancient religions, people mummified, or preserved the body (see page 9). Others, like Hindus for example, cremate the body and spread the ashes to free the soul (see page 17).

Left: Taoists believe in spirits dwelling both in Heaven and on Earth which, if venerated and worshipped, grant many favours and blessings. This statue comes from Taiwan. Images like this one can be found on many altars.

Below: a mummy from an ancient Incan burial site.

Below: lighting candles is a ritual shared by many.

Religion and state

Some countries have an official state religion which the majority of people follow and that is taught in schools. Other countries are secular (which means being concerned with worldly matters and not religious affairs). Sometimes, conflict arises if a state tries to impose its religious laws and beliefs on non-believers, or if secular and religious groups clash.

Worship and rituals

Each religion has its own rituals, or set of symbolic repeated actions which express different aspects of faith. On special occasions, such as the birth of a child or a marriage, ritual ceremonies are held to celebrate the important event. Rituals are also celebrated during festivals or on feast days when people commemorate special religious events (see pages 18–19).

Mesopotamian and Egyptian Religions

Below: a statue of the goddess Ishtar. She is wearing a skirt decorated with fish swimming in a flowing river.

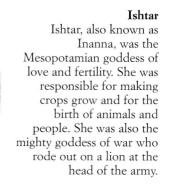

From about 7,000 years ago, two of the world's greatest civilizations developed in the Near East. One flourished in modern-day Iraq, on the fertile flood plains between the Rivers Tigris and Euphrates. This region became known as Mesopotamia, 'the land between the two rivers'. The other civilization grew in ancient Egypt, along the banks of the River Nile. The people of both civilizations worshipped a large number of gods and goddesses whom they believed controlled all aspects of the universe, nature and everyday life, including the weather, the harvest, birth and death. Among the chief gods of Mesopotamia were Enlil, Lord of the Wind, and his father Anu, Lord of Heaven. In Egypt, the most important god was Ra, the sun god. These ancient peoples believed that it was vital to obey the gods and ensure their happiness, otherwise they might send disasters such as wars, disease and floods as punishment.

Above: this terracotta head of a Mesopotamian god dates from about 2100 BCE.

Cities of the gods

The Mesopotamians built great cities, each dedicated to a god or goddess who was believed to live in the city. Magnificent stepped temples, called ziggurats, were built in the city centres, with the god's shrine at the top.

A map of Mesopotamia and some of its main cities.

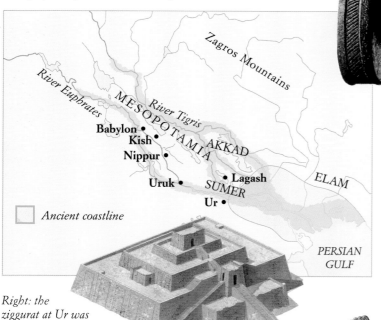

Zagros Mountains

River Euphrates

MESOPOTAMIA

River Tigris

AKKAD

Babylon •
Kish •
Nippur •

Uruk • • Lagash
SUMER
Ur •

ELAM

☐ *Ancient coastline*

PERSIAN GULF

Right: the ziggurat at Ur was built in about 2000 BCE and dedicated to the moon god Nanna and his wife Ningal.

Below: hands folded in prayer, from the figure of a priest.

Priests

Priests played an important role in Mesopotamian religions. Every day, they made offerings of food and drink to the gods and goddesses in the temple. They also presided over special feast days which were celebrated with music, dancing and the telling of stories of the great and glorious deeds performed by the gods.

Ishtar

Ishtar, also known as Inanna, was the Mesopotamian goddess of love and fertility. She was responsible for making crops grow and for the birth of animals and people. She was also the mighty goddess of war who rode out on a lion at the head of the army.

Genies and demons

The Mesopotamians believed in many lesser gods, called genies, who played a major part in their daily lives. Genies could be good or bad. Good genies, such as the eagle-headed genie, left, acted as guardian spirits, protecting people from harm and carrying their prayers to the gods. Evil genies, such as Pazuzu, right, brought death and disease, and led people to behave wickedly.

Funeral rituals

The Mesopotamians were strong believers in the afterlife. They performed funeral rituals for their rulers and built them lavish tombs, filled with precious possessions to take into the next world. This harp, left, was found in the tomb of a queen who was buried along with twenty-three attendants to look after her every need. One attendant was found with her hand on the harp.

Right: the winged demon Pazuzu was believed to live on the edge of the desert and guard the tree of life.

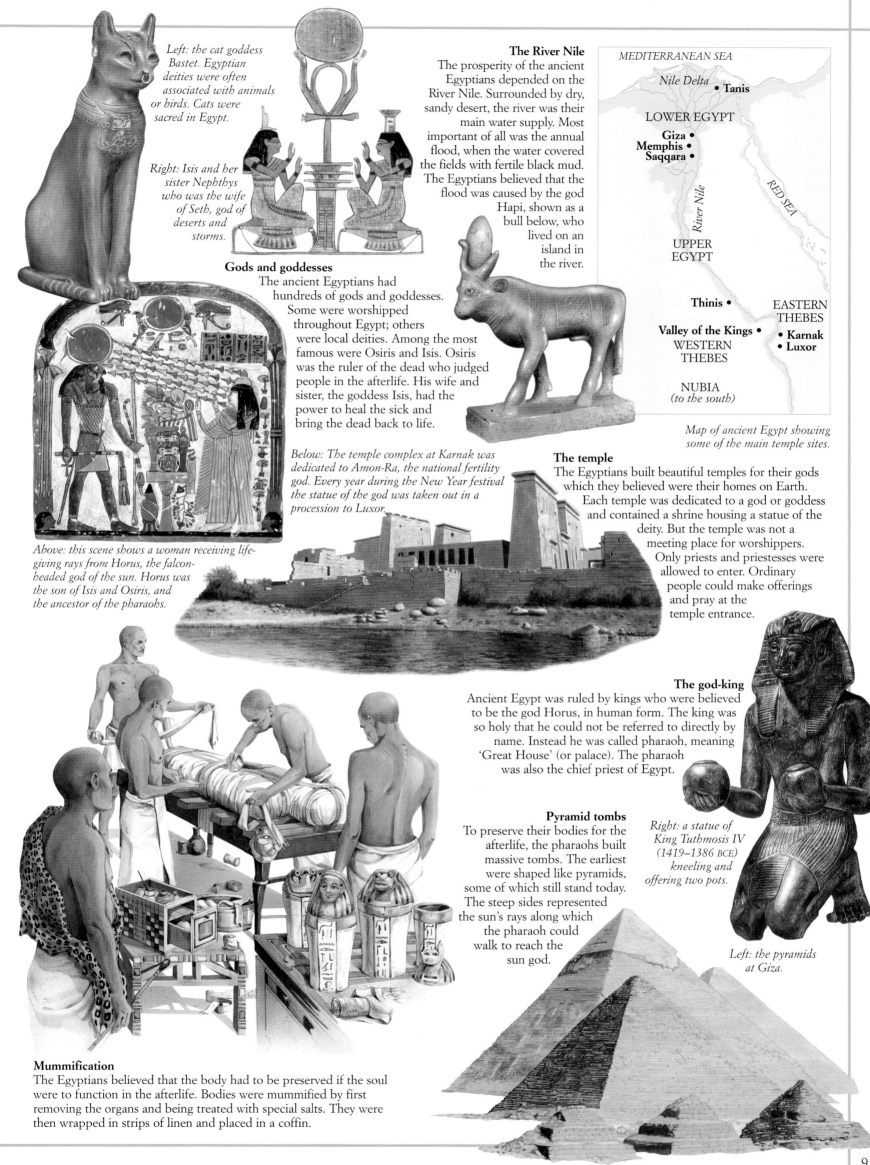

Left: the cat goddess Bastet. Egyptian deities were often associated with animals or birds. Cats were sacred in Egypt.

Right: Isis and her sister Nephthys who was the wife of Seth, god of deserts and storms.

Gods and goddesses

The ancient Egyptians had hundreds of gods and goddesses. Some were worshipped throughout Egypt; others were local deities. Among the most famous were Osiris and Isis. Osiris was the ruler of the dead who judged people in the afterlife. His wife and sister, the goddess Isis, had the power to heal the sick and bring the dead back to life.

Above: this scene shows a woman receiving life-giving rays from Horus, the falcon-headed god of the sun. Horus was the son of Isis and Osiris, and the ancestor of the pharaohs.

The River Nile

The prosperity of the ancient Egyptians depended on the River Nile. Surrounded by dry, sandy desert, the river was their main water supply. Most important of all was the annual flood, when the water covered the fields with fertile black mud. The Egyptians believed that the flood was caused by the god Hapi, shown as a bull below, who lived on an island in the river.

MEDITERRANEAN SEA
Nile Delta
• Tanis
LOWER EGYPT
Giza •
Memphis •
Saqqara •
River Nile
RED SEA
UPPER EGYPT
Thinis •
EASTERN THEBES
Valley of the Kings • • Karnak • Luxor
WESTERN THEBES
NUBIA (to the south)

Map of ancient Egypt showing some of the main temple sites.

Below: The temple complex at Karnak was dedicated to Amon-Ra, the national fertility god. Every year during the New Year festival the statue of the god was taken out in a procession to Luxor.

The temple

The Egyptians built beautiful temples for their gods which they believed were their homes on Earth. Each temple was dedicated to a god or goddess and contained a shrine housing a statue of the deity. But the temple was not a meeting place for worshippers. Only priests and priestesses were allowed to enter. Ordinary people could make offerings and pray at the temple entrance.

The god-king

Ancient Egypt was ruled by kings who were believed to be the god Horus, in human form. The king was so holy that he could not be referred to directly by name. Instead he was called pharaoh, meaning 'Great House' (or palace). The pharaoh was also the chief priest of Egypt.

Pyramid tombs

To preserve their bodies for the afterlife, the pharaohs built massive tombs. The earliest were shaped like pyramids, some of which still stand today. The steep sides represented the sun's rays along which the pharaoh could walk to reach the sun god.

Right: a statue of King Tuthmosis IV (1419–1386 BCE) kneeling and offering two pots.

Left: the pyramids at Giza.

Mummification

The Egyptians believed that the body had to be preserved if the soul were to function in the afterlife. Bodies were mummified by first removing the organs and being treated with special salts. They were then wrapped in strips of linen and placed in a coffin.

Greek and Roman Religions

The ancient Greeks had many gods and goddesses whom they believed watched over them and controlled events on Earth. In many ways, the Greeks thought of the gods as like humans – they got married, had children and displayed human emotions, such as anger, love and jealousy. But the gods were also immortal and all-powerful, and had to be respected. The most important gods were the Olympians, ruled over by Zeus. In the 2nd century CE, Greece was conquered by the Romans, who incorporated many aspects of Greek culture, including the gods, into their own. Both the Greeks and Romans were deeply superstitious. Before embarking on any new project, they always tried to discover the will of the gods by consulting oracles and interpreting omens. The most famous Greek oracle was at Delphi, where the god Apollo was believed to speak to worshippers through his priestess.

Above: Gaia, the creator of the sea and mountains.

First beings

According to Greek legend, the first beings on Earth were Gaia, the Earth goddess, and Uranos, god of the sky. They had many children, including 14 giants called the Titans. One of the Titans, Cronos, was the father of Zeus.

Right: Apollo, the sun god.

This map shows the Greek city-states in the Mediterranean and the area influenced by Greek culture.

Greek gods

The most powerful of the Greek gods were the 12 Olympians. They were believed to live on Mount Olympus, the highest mountain in Greece. From their lofty home, they ruled over the world and oversaw people's daily lives. The ruler of the gods was the mighty Zeus, above. He was married to his sister, Hera, the goddess of marriage and women, but was frequently unfaithful to her. The Olympians were closely related. Zeus's brothers were Poseidon, god of the sea, and Pluto, ruler of the Underworld. His sisters were Hestia, goddess of the hearth, and Demeter, goddess of plants and farming.

Greek influence

Lack of farmland and overcrowding at home led to colonies being established around the Mediterranean and in Asia Minor (modern Turkey). There was close contact between Greece and the colonies, and Greek ideas quickly spread.

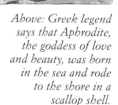

Above: Greek legend says that Aphrodite, the goddess of love and beauty, was born in the sea and rode to the shore in a scallop shell.

The temples

The Greeks built beautiful temples as the gods' homes on Earth. Inside stood a cult statue of the deity to whom the temple was dedicated. A second room housed jewellery, vases and statues offered to the gods by worshippers. Temples were built from marble and decorated outside with brightly painted scenes from mythology.

Above: a statue of the mythical monster, Medusa, from a temple in Sicily.

Ritual and sacrifice

Outside the main entrance of a Greek temple stood a stone altar. If people wanted to ask the god to grant a favour, they might take a bird or animal to the temple. There the priest sacrificed it on the altar and offered it to the god.

Right: Greek temples had elegant columns along the front and sides. These columns are built in Doric style.

The statue of the deity stood in the main room of the temple.

Above: a carving showing a priest and priestess.

Roman religion

The ancient Romans expected protection and special favours from their gods in return for worshipping them. The Romans called on certain gods for specific needs. There were gods who protected the state and gods, or guardian spirits, worshipped by families who protected their homes. One of the most important state gods was Janus, the god of doorways. He had two faces which permitted him to watch over the entrances and exits of public buildings.

Above: a coin showing the two-headed god, Janus. His symbol was a key for opening and closing doors. He was also the god of new beginnings. The first month of our year, January, is named after him.

Borrowing from the Greeks

Many of the deities of Roman state religion were adopted and adapted from the Greek gods, although they were given different names. For example, the Greek goddess of wisdom, Pallas Athena, was called Minerva in Rome. Poseidon, Greek god of the sea, became the Roman Neptune.

Right: Roman mosaic of Neptune. Like his Greek counterpart, he rode in a golden chariot and carried a trident. A festival was held in his honour in July, the driest time of the year.

Left: Renaissance painting of Pallas Athena.

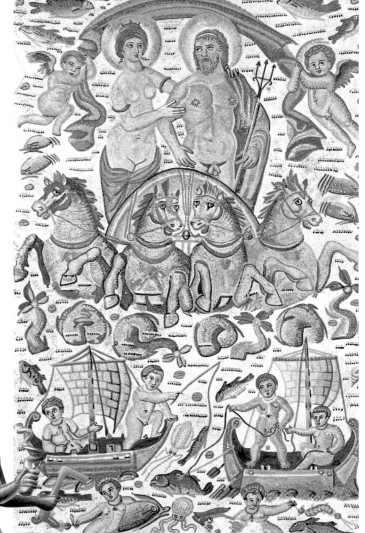

Gods and emperors

The first emperor of Rome, Augustus, used religion to strengthen his rule. To mark the start of a new, peaceful era for Rome, he founded a temple to Apollo, the god of youth and civilization. After his death, Augustus himself was declared a god, as were the rulers that followed him.

Left: this bronze statue shows the goddess Fortuna. She represented the unexpected twists and turns of fate. She was also associated with Emperor Augustus.

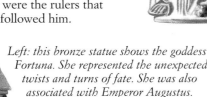

Cult of Diana

Many Romans lost faith in the formality and rituals of the state religion and did not feel it met their spiritual needs. They turned to various smaller cults instead. Diana, left, the goddess of the moon and hunting, was worshipped at shrines in Italy and Greece. At her shrine near Lake Nemi, Italy, human sacrifices sometimes took place.

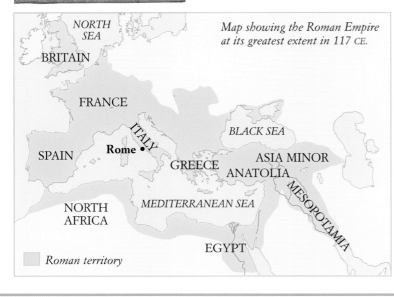

Map showing the Roman Empire at its greatest extent in 117 CE.

NORTH SEA
BRITAIN
FRANCE
ITALY
SPAIN
Rome •
GREECE
BLACK SEA
ASIA MINOR
ANATOLIA
MEDITERRANEAN SEA
MESOPOTAMIA
NORTH AFRICA
EGYPT

☐ *Roman territory*

Right: in 30 BCE, Egypt was seized by Rome. The worship of Egyptian gods, such as Anubis and Isis, continued well into Roman times. The cult of the goddess Isis became popular across the Roman Empire.

Gods from other cultures

The stone head above shows the goddess Cybele, also known as the Great Mother. Originally from Asia Minor (modern Turkey), she was one of several foreign deities introduced into Rome. Cybele was the goddess of nature, fertility and healing. Her cult was brought to Rome in 205 BCE and attracted a considerable following.

Below: the bronze head of a bull-horned god.

Celtic and Norse Religions

From the 5th century BCE to the 1st century CE Celtic peoples spread across northern and western Europe, bringing their religion with them. Although ruthless warriors, they were also fine poets and musicians. They passed down stories about their gods and heroes by word of mouth in the form of long epic poems. Each clan worshipped its own gods, and deities were also borrowed from other cultures such as Rome. The Norsemen, or Vikings, conquered many parts of northern Europe in the 8th to 11th centuries. They were warriors and seafarers from Scandinavia, the present-day countries of Denmark, Norway and Sweden. The Vikings worshipped many gods who helped them make sense of the cold, harsh world they inhabited. Their rich mythology told of the gods' exploits as they fought the forces of darkness and chaos which threatened *Midgard*, the world of humans.

The Celtic gods and heroes

The greatest god of the Celts was Dagda, the good god and the 'father of all'. He had a club that could kill nine men with one stroke, then bring them back to life again. Dagda owned a magic cauldron which never emptied and provided a never-ending feast of food and drink in the Otherworld where the gods lived. Many heroes from mythology and history mingled with the Celtic gods. They included the great giant, Bran, who walked across the Irish Sea and gave his life for his people.

Right: a bronze crown discovered in Norfolk, England. It is decorated with images of a face, probably of a deity. It may have been a ritual headdress worn by a Druid.

Left: Brigit was a great healer associated with fertility and the spring. A patron of poetry and crafts, she later became known as the Christian St. Brigid.

The Druids

Religious rituals and ceremonies were performed by priests called Druids. They acted as messengers between the worlds of the gods and humans, and so were very powerful. Sacrifices, sometimes of humans, were used to predict auspicious dates for harvest, coronations and other important events. The Druids were also judges and teachers, and passed down the history and myths of the Celts by word of mouth.

Map showing Celtic lands in Europe.

IRELAND	
BRITAIN	
	CENTRAL
GAUL	EUROPE
	ITALY
SPAIN	
	GALATIA

Celtic lands until 500 BCE
Expansion after 500 BCE
Celtiberians
Galatians

River Rhine
River Danube

Map showing Celtic lands in Europe.

Animal symbolism

Many Celtic gods were portrayed in semi-human, semi-animal form to show the close links between humans and the natural world. Animals were also important symbols. Dogs were connected with the Otherworld and were believed to have magical healing qualities. Bulls were symbols of wealth, strength and kingship.

Below: this bronze bull was buried in the grave of a Celtic chieftain in the late 1st century BCE.

Right: a bronze dog from a Celtic healing sanctuary in England.

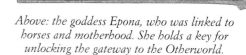

Above: the goddess Epona, who was linked to horses and motherhood. She holds a key for unlocking the gateway to the Otherworld.

Antlered gods

The image of an antlered god, right, is often seen in Celtic mythology. This god was called Cernunnos, the 'horned one'. Cernunnos was Lord of Animals, and god of crops, fruit and money. His horns symbolize strength and fighting ability. He wears or holds twisted bands of precious metals, called torcs, which show his divine nature. Accompanying him is a snake representing fertility and regrowth.

Norse gods

The Vikings believed that their gods lived in magnificent halls in a heavenly place called *Asgard*. A rainbow bridge connected *Asgard* to *Midgard*, the human world. Below this came *Niflheim*, the land of the dead. *Asgard* was ruled by Odin, king of the gods. Legend says that he gave up the sight of one eye to gain wisdom and knowledge. Odin's son, Thor, was the god of thunder who rode across the sky in his chariot, wielding his magic hammer, Mjollnir. One of the most important gods associated with earth and water was Frey, the god of fertility. Frey made the land fruitful and granted peace to worshippers.

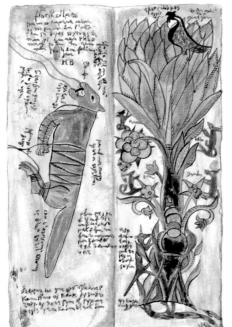

Left: Thor was famous for his fiery temper, incredible strength and his battles against the giants, the arch-enemies of the gods.

Above: this 12th-century tapestry from Skog in Sweden shows three figures thought to be Odin, Thor and Frey.

Left: the trickster Loki, who was tied across three sharp rocks as punishment for causing the god Balder's death. At Ragnarok, he was to break free from his bounds and join the giants in the attack on Asgard.

Ragnarok

The Vikings believed in a final battle, called Ragnarok, or the Doom of the Gods. In this battle, the gods and their arch-enemies, the giants, would fight and destroy each other. This would be the final struggle between the forces of good and evil, and would herald the end of the world. Out of the destruction would rise a new world in which everyone would live in peace and harmony.

Left: the monstrous wolf Fenrir (Loki's son), was chained to a large rock so that he could not escape. The Vikings believed that, at Ragnarok, Fenrir would break his chains and devour the great god, Odin.

Map showing Viking lands 800–1000 CE.

ICELAND

KINGDOM OF SCOTS   NORWAY   SWEDEN

IRISH KINGDOMS

KINGDOM OF YORK   DENMARK

Normandy

▢ Danish Viking settlements
▢ Norwegian Viking settlements
▢ Swedish Viking settlements

Memorial stones

The Vikings believed in life after death, and buried their dead with their possessions to accompany them into the next life. Some people set up stones, like the one on the right, to remember a dead friend or relative. The fearsome image on the stone was intended to keep evil spirits away.

Left: this stone shows a dead hero arriving in Valhalla, Odin's Hall of the Slain in Asgard. *Here the warriors spent their time fighting and feasting.*

Conversion to Christianity

During the 9th and 10th centuries, Christian missionaries spread through western Europe, preaching their beliefs. They eventually reached Scandinavia, eager to convert the Vikings. By the 11th century, Scandinavia had become Christian. For many years, the old and new religions existed side by side. But gradually many Viking customs, such as burying grave goods, were outlawed, and Christian churches, made from wood, were built all over Scandinavia.

Above: even after they became Christians, Viking craftsmen kept their own distinct styles, as this gold crucifix shows.

Hindu History and Beliefs

Hinduism is one of the world's oldest religions, although we have no fixed date for when it began. Its roots reach back roughly 4,500 years to the time of the great Indus Valley civilization that flourished along the banks of the River Indus in north-west India (now Pakistan). Archaeologists have discovered many clay figures of gods and goddesses from this time that are similar to those worshipped by Hindus today. In about 1500 BCE, the Indus Valley civilization collapsed and a nomadic group of people called the Aryans began to invade north-west India. Their religious ideas mixed with those of the Indus Valley to form the basis of Hinduism as it is practised today. Hindus do not call their code of beliefs 'Hinduism', a term coined in the 19th century. They call it *sanatana dharma,* which means eternal law or teaching. Today, there are about 800 million Hindus, many of whom live in India. Many more have settled overseas, in countries such as Britain and the United States, where they have taken their beliefs with them.

Map of the Indian subcontinent showing the Indus Valley.

Left: mother goddesses from the Indus Valley.

Left: hundreds of stone seals have been found in the Indus Valley. They were used by merchants to mark their bundles of goods. Many show animals, such as horned bulls or tigers, or religious scenes.

The Indus Valley
By 2500 BCE, the Indus Valley civilization had reached the peak of its powers and was the largest empire in the ancient world. This highly sophisticated society was centred around two great cities – Harappa and Mohenjo-Daro. Archaeologists began excavating the cities in the 1920s. Among the artefacts they found was the carved stone head, left. It may have been the head of a king or a priest with his eyes closed in meditation.

The religion of the Vedas
The Aryans worshipped many gods associated with nature and the world around them. They performed elaborate rituals to keep the gods happy so they would grant favours, such as a good harvest. Our main source of information about Aryan religion is the *Rig Veda*, a collection of hymns recited by the priests. The *Rig Veda* remains one of the most sacred texts of Hinduism.

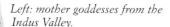

Left: a painted floor plan showing the way to the sacred shrine of the deity in a Hindu temple.

Right: Agni, the god of fire, was one of the most popular Aryan deities. He acted as a messenger between the gods and human beings.

Pilgrimages
Millions of Hindus make pilgrimages every year, to sacred places such as temples, mountains and rivers. The purpose of the visit may be to thank the gods for granting a wish or to pray for something special, like the birth of a child. Hindus also believe that making a pilgrimage takes them closer to *moksha*, or salvation from the endless cycle of birth, death and rebirth.

Below: the Mukteswar Temple in Bhubaneswar, Orissa, dates from the 10th century and is dedicated to the great god Shiva. The tall tower, or shikara, *stands over the central shrine. It represents the link between Earth and Heaven.*

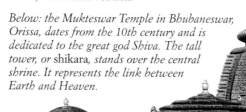

HINDUISM

Origins Hinduism evolved in India about 1500 BCE.

Beliefs By leading a good life, a person can be released from the cycle of reincarnation and achieve union with God.

Adherents About 800 million.

Sacred texts *Vedas, Upanishads, Brahmanas, Puranas* and epics (including *Ramayana* and *Mahabharata)*, *Tantras* and the writings of revered gurus.

Temples
Hindus worship in temples, or *mandirs*, each of which is dedicated to a particular god, goddess or holy man. A temple is considered the deity's home on Earth and the deity's presence is shown by an image which stands in a shrine in the innermost, and most sacred, part of the temple. Hindus visit the temple for a *darshana*, or viewing, of the deity.

The Trimurti

Hindus believe in a great soul or spirit, called Brahman, or God. Brahman has no shape or form and cannot be seen but is present in everything. Each of the thousands of Hindu deities represents an aspect of Brahman. The three most important gods are the *trimurti*, or trinity – Brahma, the creator of the universe; Vishnu, the protector; and Shiva, the destroyer. Vishnu and Shiva are very popular gods, with millions of followers and temples all over India. Brahma is not widely worshipped and has only one temple.

Left: this painting shows Vishnu and his consort, Lakshmi, resting on the coils of a sacred snake. From Vishnu's navel, Brahma is born, sitting in a lotus blossom.

Above: Shiva is a god of opposites. From time to time, he destroys the universe so it can be created again. He is often shown dancing; as he dances, he reconciles destruction and creation, darkness and light, day and night. Underfoot he treads the dwarf of ignorance.

Vishnu's avatars

From time to time, Hindus believe, Vishnu appears in the world in an earthly incarnation, known as an *avatar*. He comes to Earth to save the world from evil or bring about good. Nine of ten *avatars* have already appeared. The most important are the gods Rama and Krishna. The tenth *avatar*, Kalki, the rider on a white horse, is yet to come.

Right: many stories are told about Krishna, one of the most popular Hindu gods. He is usually shown with black or blue skin, playing a flute.

Above: Saraswati is the consort, or wife, of Lord Brahma and goddess of learning, music and the arts. She is often shown holding a book and a vina *(a type of musical instrument).*

Left: the elephant-headed god, Ganesha, is the son of Lord Shiva and his consort, Parvati. One of the most popular Hindu gods, he is worshipped at the start of new ventures, such as beginning a journey or moving house.

Goddesses

Like many Hindu deities, the goddess Durga is a mixture of kindness and cruelty, life and death, good and evil. She is shown in many forms, including the terrifying Kali, above. Although Kali is depicted as a ferocious figure with a necklace of skulls and her tongue dripping blood, she is worshipped with great devotion. She represents the the more frightening aspects of life, such as the passage of time and death.

Sacred cows

In Hinduism, cows are sacred and cannot be harmed or killed. Most Hindus will not eat beef. This is because cows are givers of milk, one of the most precious sources of food, and are associated with Krishna. This figure, right, is the cow goddess, Kamadhenu, who symbolizes prosperity and who gives milk to the gods and the sages.

The story of Rama

Rama, the seventh *avatar* of Vishnu, is the hero of the great epic poem the *Ramayana*. The poem tells how Rama, son of the king of Ayodhya, was banished to the forest where his wife, Sita, is kidnapped by Ravana, an evil demon king. Rama rescues Sita, kills Ravana, and returns home to be crowned king. Rama is worshipped as the ideal human being, courageous, wise and loyal, who helps good triumph over evil.

Right: statue from Tamil Nadu showing the coronation of Rama.

Practising Hinduism

About eight out of ten people in India describe themselves as Hindus but the way in which they practise their religion varies greatly from region to region. Hinduism is not a fixed, formal religion with firm rules and beliefs, but a way of life which affects everything a Hindu does, from cooking a meal, to going to school, to working in an office. Hindus try to live their lives according to a code of behaviour called *dharma*. This means doing their duty to their family and friends, helping their neighbours, being kind to others and telling the truth. Despite their differences, the various Hindu traditions have many beliefs in common. One of these beliefs is reincarnation, which means that when a person dies their soul is reborn again in another body. Their next life is dictated by the good or bad deeds in present life, and by their results, known as *karma*. The goal of a Hindu's spiritual life is to break free of the cycle of birth, death and rebirth, and to achieve *moksha*, or ultimate salvation.

Above: the sacred symbol Aum (Om) is spoken at the beginning and end of every prayer, and during meditation. According to the scriptures, it was the first sound, out of which the rest of the world was created.

Above: this woman is carrying a portable shrine containing an image of Bhairava, a form of the god Shiva.

Honouring the deities

Apart from the three main deities of the *trimurti* (see previous page), Hindus worship thousands of lesser gods and goddesses. Some are worshipped all over India. Others are associated with a particular village, or even with a family. They include spirits which are believed to watch over the village and to bring ruin unless they are treated with respect.

Right: a statue of a village god, from Tamil Nadu, in southern India.

Left: an image of Karumari Amman, a popular village goddess from southern India.

Below: this sacred horse figure from Tamil Nadu is the guardian spirit of a village. It is accompanied by brave warriors who watch over the villagers.

PAKISTAN
NEPAL
INDIA   BANGLADESH
MYANMAR

Tamil Nadu

SRI LANKA
MALAYSIA

Hindu majority
Hindu minority
Hindu presence
INDONESIA

Map showing the density of Hindu population in Asia.

Left: fire plays a key part in Hindu worship. It acts as a messenger between the gods and humans, and also removes evil. In this purification ceremony, a woman holds two dishes of flames while another is placed on her head.

Above: a representation of the footprints of the great god Vishnu, which symbolize his divine presence on Earth. The cult of Vishnu is quite popular.

Hindu worship

Many Hindus visit the *mandir* (temple) to worship but many also perform their daily worship, called *puja*, at home. They set aside a room or part of a room for a shrine with an image of the family's favourite deity. *Puja* begins with the recitation of prayers, called *mantras*, from the sacred texts, and is followed by the offering of gifts, such as flowers, fruit and sweet foods. These are presented to the deity in return for his or her blessing.

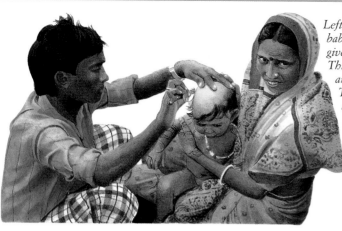

Left: before a Hindu baby is a year old, it is given its first haircut. This is said to remove any bad karma. The hair is burned as an offering to the gods. A prayer is said to wish the baby a long, happy life.

Left: when a Hindu boy is about ten years old, he goes through the sacred text ceremony. This marks the end of his childhood and the start of his adult life.

Rites of passage

Traditionally, a Hindu's life is divided into four stages, called *ashramas*. These are: *brahmacharya*, or life as a student; *grihasta*, or married life; *vanaprastha*, or retirement; and *sannyasin*, or renouncing worldly life. At each stage, there are particular duties to be carried out. The special times in life, such as being born, getting married and dying, are marked with ceremonies, called *samskaras*, held in front of a sacred fire. Traditionally, there are 16 *samskaras*. They begin even before a baby is born with prayers for its health and future.

Right: when a Hindu dies, his or her body is cremated on a funeral pyre. If possible, the ashes are collected and scattered in the sacred River Ganges.

Left: marriage is one of the most important stages in a Hindu's life. In traditional families, the parents find a suitable husband or wife for their children. The wedding ceremony is elaborate and many rituals are performed. This young girl is dressed for her wedding day.

Religious paths

In Hinduism, there are four main paths or ways of reaching *moksha*. Each person must choose the path which suits him or her best. The four paths are *bhakti* (devotion), *jnana* (knowledge), *karma* (action) and *yoga* (meditation). Hindus who follow *bhakti* devote themselves to a personal god, such as Krishna or Rama. Followers of *jnana* try to find the true meaning of life through learning and study. *Karma* means action and its results. Followers of *karma* try to act selflessly, without thought for their own reward. Some Hindus use *yoga* and meditation, right, to train their bodies and minds, and bring them closer to *moksha*.

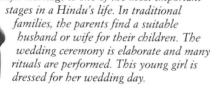

Below: in some parts of India, the Dussehra festival celebrates Rama's victory over Ravana, as told in the Ramayana. *The story is acted out with processions and plays.*

Dance and drama

Dance and drama play an important part in Hindu religious celebrations. Many dances and plays are inspired by stories from legends and myths. At festival times, actors travel from village to village, performing stories or retelling them in dance. These forms of entertainment are extremely popular. Classical Indian dance follows strict rules, set down thousands of years ago. The two leading dance traditions are *Bharat Natya* and *Kathakali*. *Kathakali* is only done by men who wear fantastic masks and costumes to perform dances based on episodes from the great epic poems.

Right: a Bharat Natya *dancer. In Indian classical dance, each movement of the hands, head and eyes has a special meaning. They indicate an emotion or part of the plot.*

Below: this wooden snake mask is worn in some dances to chase away the evil spirits that cause sickness. In Hinduism, sacred snakes are believed to protect people from evil.

Festivals

Although most festivals of the Hindu calendar, such as Holi and Diwali, are celebrated by all Hindus all over the world (see page 19), there are also many local festivals dedicated to particular deities. Rituals and practices differ from place to place. Festival celebrations may take place in the home or at the temple where the congregation gathers together to read the sacred texts and perform rituals. Some festivals are celebrated with processions.

Parades

Some festivals are celebrated with spectacular street parades and pageants. These rituals are performed to honour deities or to present sacred objects to worshippers. Pageants include the re-enactment of the deeds of founders and teachers. Some parades or processions are also held in special times of need when worshippers call on God or the gods for their help.

Right: in August, a special procession takes place in Kandy, Sri Lanka. Beautifully decorated elephants parade through the city, one of which carries a casket containing a precious relic – a sacred tooth said to have belonged to the Buddha himself.

Above: during the Christian celebration of Carnival, many dress up in costumes and participate in parades before beginning the season of Lent, a time of fasting and prayer.

Religious Feast Days

Feast days and festivals are an important part of every religion and system of beliefs. Festivals are times of celebration, when members of a faith mark a special occasion with services and ceremonies, prayers and parades, food, music and dancing. Apart from being joyful occasions, they also provide an opportunity for members of a faith to join together as a group and to feel closer to God, friends and family. Some religious festivals have their roots in ancient times and celebrate critical times of the year, such as the gathering of the harvest before winter begins, the coming of the new year or the changing seasons. Other festivals celebrate important events in a religion's history or in the lives of its gods, founders and teachers.

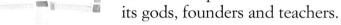

Music and dance

In some religions, music and dance are used as a form of celebration. Some worshippers sing hymns and songs to praise and thank God. Other cultures use dance as a way of communicating with the gods and spirits. The Ashanti and Dogon peoples of West Africa include music and dance in their funeral rites. The Ashanti believe that a dead person's soul takes five days to climb a hill to Heaven. During this time, mourners fast and sing songs to show their grief. Dogon dancers, like the one shown on the left, wear elaborate masks and dye their costumes red to symbolize death.

Lighting candles

Many rituals and celebrations include the lighting of candles, lamps and lanterns. These lights are used on festive and solemn occasions. For many, light is a symbol of the divine presence of a deity. A burning candle or lamp can also be lit as an offering.

Above: during Easter, Christians remember Jesus's death on the Cross and his Resurrection. Candles, such as the one held by this boy, are lit to symbolize the risen Jesus.

Left: a dancer from Papua New Guinea dressed in ceremonial costume.

Right: Wooden drums are beaten at many African festivals to help dancers keep their rhythm. Sometimes the drums become sacred objects in their own right.

Dressing up

Many worshippers dress up in special clothing for ceremonies. Colourful clothing and costumes add to the festivity of many celebrations. These children (above), have dressed up to celebrate Hanamatsuri, the Japanese flower festival, which marks the birth of the Buddha. They place flowers on a shrine to celebrate the Buddha's birth in a beautiful garden.

Festival foods

Some religions observe feast days by fasting (skipping meals) or by not eating certain foods. Fasting, for some worshippers, helps to cleanse the spirit. For others, festivals can also be a time for cooking and eating delicious foods. Many dishes have a special significance and are only eaten at festival times. On the left, a Jewish father is helping his daughter to make a loaf of *challah* bread. This is eaten on *Shabbat*, the Jewish holy day, and during other Jewish festivals. The loaves are braided to remind the Jews of God, the *Torah* (their sacred book) and the holy land of Israel.

Right: a gingerbread house baked for Christmas in Germany.

Left: Loaves of challah bread are baked before Shabbat because no baking or other work is allowed on the holy day itself.

Left: many special foods are cooked at Chinese New Year to bring good luck in the coming year. For example, noodles are said to ensure long life. The treats on this plate, called a 'Tray of Togetherness', symbolize happiness, prosperity and good health.

Prayer and meditation

Some feast days are special days reserved for prayer and reflection. Feast days can bring congregations together to pray or they can also be a time for personal spiritual growth.

Right: some Muslims spend the night of Laylat ul-Qadr, or the Night of Power, praying and reading the Qur'an, the holy book. Muslims remember the first time that Allah revealed the words of the Qur'an to the Prophet Muhammad.

Decorating the home

Decorations serve as visual reminders of the importance of feast days. They help to create a festive atmosphere which makes feast days so special. Some people decorate their homes both inside and out. Many different kinds of materials can be used, such as flowers, branches, fruit, lights, banners and flags. These decorations serve as symbols to help worshippers recall important historical events or religious truths.

Right: lighting candles at Hanukkah reminds Jews of how God miraculously kept the Temple lamp burning for eight days, even though there was only enough oil left to last for a single day.

Above: at the festival of Diwali, Hindus decorate their homes with diva *lights and make offerings to the deities in the* mandir *(temple). The* divas *are lit to guide the god Rama home from exile and to welcome Lakshmi, goddess of wealth and good fortune, into people's homes.*

Giving gifts

The ritual of exchanging gifts is shared by many religions. Gifts and cards exchanged at festivals have special symbolism. For some, they remind worshippers of God's, or a god's, generosity and kindness. Giving gifts can also be a gesture of love and goodwill from one person to another. As gestures of peace, gifts can bring people of different religions together.

Left: at Easter, many Christians give Easter eggs, as symbols of new life. This beautifully decorated egg was presented by Tsar Nicholas II of Russia to his wife at Easter 1895.

Right: during the festival of Holi, in spring, Hindus play practical jokes on each other, including drenching each other with coloured water to remind them of the god Krishna's mischievous childhood.

Celebrating the seasons

Since ancient times people have celebrated the changing of the seasons, which are especially important times for farmers. Each festival has its own deep religious significance. Feast days during spring celebrate nature's renewal. It is a time of hope and spiritual awakening. During harvest festivals in the autumn, worshippers give thanks and rejoice over the fruits that the Earth has provided.

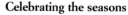

The Life and the Way of the Buddha

Above: this carving shows Queen Maya's dream of a white elephant before Siddhartha was born.

Below: this picture shows Siddhartha leaving home. So that no one would hear him going, the gods muffled the sounds of his horse's hooves.

Buddhism began in north-eastern India about 2,500 years ago. It is based on the teachings of an Indian nobleman, Siddhartha Gautama, who became the Buddha, or 'Enlightened One'. Siddhartha was born after his mother, Queen Maya, dreamed of a pure white elephant. He was brought up in great luxury, shielded from the problems of the outside world. Then, at the age of 29, he had an experience of suffering that changed his life. According to legend, on a secret chariot ride, Siddhartha saw a sick man, an old man and a dead man. Then he saw a holy man who, despite being poor, was happy and content. Siddhartha vowed to give up his privileged life and to follow the holy man's example. He decided to leave home and begin his search for the truth.

BUDDHISM

Origins Siddhartha Gautama, the Buddha, founded Buddhism in northern India in the fifth or sixth century BCE.

Beliefs By following the Buddha's teachings, one can achieve Enlightenment and be freed from the cycle of reincarnation.

Main subdivisions *Mahayana, Theravada, Vajrayana* and *Lamaism* (Tibetan).

Adherents about 360 million.

Sacred texts The *Tripitaka* (accepted by all Buddhists). Each subdivision also has its own sacred texts.

The search for truth
In his search for truth, Siddhartha spent many years travelling around northern India. For six years, he lived as an ascetic, fasting and meditating in the forest. It was a very tough life. Siddhartha, right, ate so little that he grew weak and thin, and almost died from hunger.

The Buddha's Enlightenment
Leaving the forest, Siddhartha made his way to the village of Bodh Gaya. There he sat down to meditate under a spreading tree. During the night, Mara, the evil one, tried to tempt Siddhartha from his quest. But Siddhartha defeated Mara and finally realized the truth. From then on, he became the Buddha, which means 'Enlightened One'.

Above: the Buddha and his first four followers.

The Buddha's teachings
After his Enlightenment, the Buddha lived as a monk, teaching what he had learned. He taught that people suffered because they always wanted more. The way out of suffering was to follow the Middle Path between great luxury and great hardship. This would lead to enlightenment and the perfect peace of *nirvana*.

Above: the sacred Bodhi tree, under which the Buddha sat, is a symbolic representation of his Enlightenment.

Right: an image of the Buddha, showing his elongated earlobes. They showed that he came from a noble family, which meant he had worn heavy earrings.

Left: the Buddha's teaching, or dharma, *is often represented by the symbol of a wheel.*

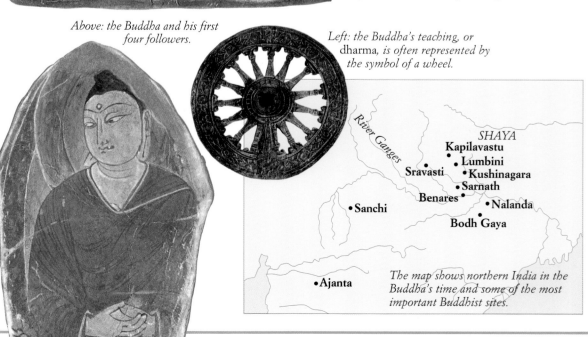

The map shows northern India in the Buddha's time and some of the most important Buddhist sites.

SHAYA
Kapilavastu
• Lumbini
Sravasti • Kushinagara
• Sarnath
Benares •
• Nalanda
• Sanchi
Bodh Gaya
• Ajanta
River Ganges

Branches of Buddhism

About a hundred years after the Buddha's death, differences arose between the groups of monks about the Buddha's teachings. As a result, Buddhism split into two schools of thought. *Theravada*, or 'Way of the Elders', and *Mahayana*, or 'Great Vehicle'. Gradually, *Theravada* Buddhism spread out of India to Sri Lanka, Thailand, Cambodia, Laos and Myanmar. *Mahayana* Buddhism spread north-east to Nepal, Tibet, China, Japan, Vietnam and the Korean peninsula.

Left: the Ananda stupa (temple) in Pagan, Myanmar, was built in the 11th century.

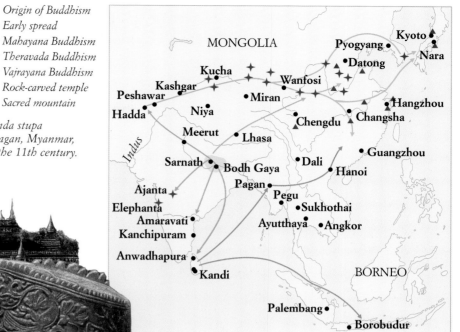

| Origin of Buddhism |
| Early spread |
| Mahayana Buddhism |
| Theravada Buddhism |
| Vajrayana Buddhism |
| ✦ Rock-carved temple |
| ▲ Sacred mountain |

Map showing the spread of Buddhism in Asia and many sacred sites.

Sacred texts

The Buddha's teachings were only written down in the first century BCE. The oldest texts are the *Pali Canon*, or *Tipitaka*, sacred to *Theravada* Buddhists. *Mahayana* Buddhists have their own texts, called *sutras*.

Left: a head of the Buddha from Cambodia, a Theravada *Buddhist country.*

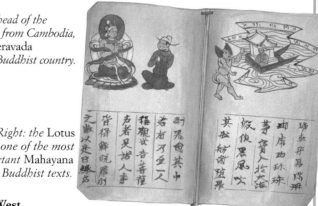

Right: the Lotus Sutra, *one of the most important* Mahayana *Buddhist texts.*

Above: a design called a mandala, *used in Tibetan Buddhism to aid meditation.*

Buddhism in Tibet

Buddhism reached Tibet from India in the seventh century CE. It combined a type of *Mahayana* Buddhism with the magic and rituals of Tantric belief. The best known Tibetan Buddhists are the *Gelupka* group, or Yellow Hats. Their leader is the Dalai Lama (see page 27). Until the Chinese invasion of Tibet in 1950, the Dalai Lama was the country's religious leader and head of the government. He now lives in exile in India.

Right: many Tibetan monasteries were destroyed by the Chinese. However, a few new monasteries have been built.

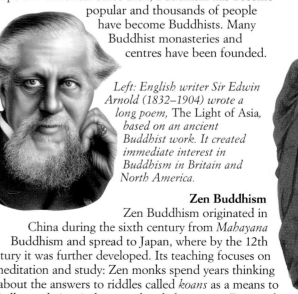

Buddhism in the West

Buddhism reached the West at the end of the 19th century, through the writings of Western scholars and their translations of ancient Buddhist texts. It was also spread by people from Buddhist countries who settled in Europe and America. Since then, Buddhism has become popular and thousands of people have become Buddhists. Many Buddhist monasteries and centres have been founded.

Left: English writer Sir Edwin Arnold (1832–1904) wrote a long poem, The Light of Asia, *based on an ancient Buddhist work. It created immediate interest in Buddhism in Britain and North America.*

Below: a Zen nun from the United States.

Zen Buddhism

Zen Buddhism originated in China during the sixth century from *Mahayana* Buddhism and spread to Japan, where by the 12th century it was further developed. Its teaching focuses on meditation and study: Zen monks spend years thinking about the answers to riddles called *koans* as a means to challenge their minds to reach enlightenment. During the second half of the 20th century teachers from Japan and Korea have brought Zen to the West. Today there are many Zen communities in North America and Europe.

Images of the Buddha

At first, the Buddha was not shown in person but by symbols, such as a wheel, a bodhi tree or a footprint. Later many different styles of Buddhist art developed. Legend tells how the statue of the two-headed Buddha, shown on the right, was created. Two Chinese pilgrims loved the Buddha with all their hearts and dreamed of having an image of him. But both were so poor that they could not afford an image each so they only had one made. To show his compassion and generosity, the Buddha divided the image in two.

Sacred places

The beautifully carved gateway, right, guarded the Great Stupa at Sanchi in India. Dating from the first century CE, it is decorated with Buddhist symbols and scenes but there are no images of the Buddha. Stupas are dome-shaped monuments which represent the Buddhist universe. They were originally built to house sacred relics belonging to the Buddha or to other teachers and monks.

Right: the Samantabhadra bodhisattva, who represents Buddhist law, is seated on an elephant holding a scroll of the scriptures.

Left and below: Dakinis are goddesses in Tibetan Buddhism who accompany other heavenly beings. They are often shown dancing, holding a magic staff.

Left: the bodhisattva Avalokiteshvara not only guides people towards enlightenment but helps them overcome their daily problems.

Heavenly beings

The Buddha did not claim to be a god and did not want to be worshipped as one. But some Buddhists worship god-like beings called *bodhisattvas*. These are perfect, heavenly figures who have gained enlightenment and could now enter *nirvana*. Instead, they choose to stay in the world and help other people to gain enlightenment for themselves. One of the most popular *bodhisattvas* is Avalokiteshvara, who represents perfect compassion.

The goddess Tara

Like all *bodhisattvas,* the White Tara is worshipped for her great compassion. She symbolizes purity and knowledge beyond human existence. According to legend, she was born out of one of the eyes of Avalokiteshvara. She is usually represented with a third eye on her forehead and an eye in each palm.

Left: the goddess Tara. With her right hand she makes a gesture symbolic of charity and sincerity, while with her left hand she forms the circle of perfection.

Above: a celestial being called a gandharva. *Gandharvas are heavenly musicians.*

The Buddha to come

Buddhists believe that the next Buddha to appear on Earth will be Maitreya. At present, he lives in a celestial realm called the *Tusita* Heaven. He will live there until Buddhism declines in thousands of years' time. It is thought that his time on Earth will herald a golden age.

Right: a Korean bronze figure of a seated Maitreya from the seventh century CE.

Buddhist Beliefs and Practice

Below: monks help the community by teaching in local schools.

Buddhists follow a system of thoughts and beliefs based on the Buddha's teachings, or *dharma*. The Buddha taught that everyone must realize the truth for him or herself. His teachings were only meant as a guide for them to follow. Buddhists believe that the *dharma* is one of the Three Jewels of Buddhism, along with the Buddha himself and the *sangha*, or Buddhist community. They are called 'jewels' because they are so precious. Buddhists commit themselves to the Three Jewels as their guides through life. Buddhists also agree to follow five basic rules, called the Five Precepts. They promise: not to kill or harm living things; not to steal; not to lie; to abstain from sexual misconduct and to avoid drugs and alcohol. Like Hindus, Buddhists believe in *karma*, the law of cause and effect, and in reincarnation. Good actions lead to a better rebirth, closer to *nirvana*. Bad deeds lead to being born further away from *nirvana*. Escaping from the cycle of birth and rebirth, and reaching the perfect peace and happiness of *nirvana* is the ultimate aim of every Buddhist's life. To achieve this, they try to follow the Buddha's teachings and develop the qualities of compassion, loving kindness and generosity in their lives.

Right: a monk covering his face with a palm leaf, according to an ancient custom in Sri Lanka.

Buddhist monks

After his Enlightenment, the Buddha lived as a monk. Many Buddhists follow his example and live as monks or nuns. They leave their homes and worldly goods behind them and dedicate their lives to practising, studying and teaching the *dharma*. The monastic life is a hard one. Monks have very few possessions and follow a strict set of rules. Many are dependent on the local Buddhist community for their food and daily needs.

Right: a young monk at his ordination in Cambodia. He is wearing saffron robes and has shaved his head, to show that he has cut his ties with the world.

Practice and meditation

Many Buddhists visit their local *vihara*, or temple, to pay their respects to the Buddha. In the shrine room, they make offerings of flowers, candles and incense before an image of the Buddha. They also recite their commitment to the Three Jewels and the Five Precepts, and take gifts for the monks. Meditation is a very important part of Buddhist practice. By meditating, Buddhists hope to calm and clear their minds and gain true knowledge, just as the Buddha did.

Right: a dancer wearing a macabre mask during a dance in a temple in Ladakh.

Buddhist festivals

Many Buddhist festivals take place during the year. The most important celebrate special times in the Buddha's life, such as his birthday or Enlightenment. Others mark the beginning of the new year, or events from Buddhist history. Celebrations vary from country to country, often incorporating local customs and traditions. At festival times, many Buddhists visit their local *vihara* to honour the Buddha. Many festive rituals also include prayer, meditation and procession.

Above: a man making an offering of incense.

Right: a Buddhist monk hoists prayer flags to celebrate Losar, the Tibetan New Year.

Jainism

The Jain religion was founded in India in the sixth century BCE by a man called Vardhamana Mahavira, the 'Great Hero'. Like the Buddha, his contemporary, Mahavira renounced his privileged life to become a wandering beggar. Dissatisfied with the teachings of other religions, including Hinduism, he spent 12 years fasting and meditating, in search of perfect knowledge. Finally, he achieved enlightenment and devoted the rest of his life to teaching others about his beliefs. By the time of his death, at the age of 72, he had gained many followers in western India. Today there are about four million Jains, most of whom live in India.

Jain beliefs

Like Hindus and Buddhists, Jains believe in the cycle of birth, death and rebirth. But they believe that the main source of bad *karma* is attachment to the material things in life and negative emotions, like greed or anger, which weigh the soul down. Good deeds, self-control, and a simple life can help wash bad *karma* away and allow the liberated soul, or *siddha* (represented by the empty silhouette above), to rise to the highest point in the universe.

Above: Mahavira gave his first sermon on a circular structure called a samavasarama.

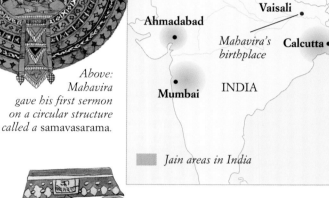

Mahavira's birthplace

Vaisali

Ahmadabad

Calcutta

Mumbai   INDIA

☐ *Jain areas in India*

Right: an illustration from a Jain manuscript shows the chakras, *or wheels, of the human body. They are considered to be the areas of the body where the soul and the body affect each other. They are also the areas where energy is focused.*

Right: the eighth Tirthankara, *Chandraprabha, the Lord of the Moon. Tradition says that he was born after his mother swallowed the moon.*

The *Tirthankaras*

Jains do not believe in a god but worship 24 spiritual teachers, called *Tirthankaras*, or 'ford-makers', who guide them through their lives. These are beings who have overcome attachment to the world and achieved enlightenment. Mahavira was the last and greatest *Tirthankara*. The *Tirthankaras* are also known as *Jinas* or 'Conquerors', from which Jains take their name.

The Five Great Vows

Jain monks and nuns promise to keep Five Great Vows to help them achieve enlightenment. These are *ahimsa*, not harming any living thing; *satya*, telling the truth; *asteya*, not stealing; *brahmacharya*, abstaining from sexual activity; and *aparigraha*, giving up attachment to worldly goods and wealth. The belief in *ahimsa* means that Jains are strict vegetarians because they believe that every living thing, however small, has a soul and should not be harmed.

Above: this devout Jain is wearing a mask so that he does not accidentally swallow any insects and kill them.

Jain temples

Jain temples are very beautiful buildings decorated with rich carvings in honour of the sacred images of the *Tirthankaras* found inside. Worshippers pour offerings of milk, yogurt, sugar and flowers over the images. Jain temples also contain images of goddesses, who are linked to the *Tirthankaras*. They include the Jain mother goddess, Ambika, above. Legend says that she gave alms to a monk, then leaped into a well to escape from her angry husband. She was later reborn as a goddess.

Left: a terracotta figure of a village deity of Jain origin, Isakai Amman, from southern India.

Right: this page from a Jain manuscript shows the Hindu god Indra with Mahavira's earthly mother, Trisala.

Sikhism

The Sikh religion began in the 15th century CE in the Punjab, an area of modern Pakistan and north-west India. At that time, the two main religions in India were Hinduism and Islam. Many people disliked the deep divisions between the two and felt excluded from them. Sikhism's founder, Guru Nanak, preached that people should be tolerant of all religions, love God and remember him in everything they do. Guru Nanak also taught that in order to love God, you must love other people. A key Sikh belief is *seva*, or 'service'. This means being kind to others and sharing what you have with them. Most of the world's 23 million Sikhs still live in the Punjab. There are also large Sikh communities in the United States and Britain.

SIKHISM

Origins Sikhism was founded during the late 15th century in the Punjab area of northern India by Guru Nanak (1469–1538)

Beliefs Sikhs believe in one God and follow the teachings of 10 gurus (teachers) who lived during the 15th to 17th centuries.

Adherents about 23 million.

Sacred texts *Guru Granth Sahib* (or *Adi Granth*).

The Gurus

The founder of the Sikh religion was a holy man called Guru Nanak (1469–1539) (above). He was the first of ten gurus, or teachers. Sikhs believe that God made his will known through these teachers and through the *Guru Granth Sahib*, the Sikh holy book. Each of the gurus made their own contribution to the Sikh faith. The fourth guru, Guru Ram Das (1534–1581) founded the city of Amritsar in the Punjab where the Sikhs' holiest shrine, the Golden Temple, or *Harimandir*, right, stands.

Below: at a special initiation ceremony Sikhs become full members of the Khalsa, *a community of Sikhs who vow to defend their religion.*

Left: during Sikh services and ceremonies, an appointed reader, called a granthi, *reads from the* Guru Granth Sahib.

Below: a Sikh carves sacred verses written in Gurmukhi into stone.

The Five Ks

Devout Sikhs wear five symbols of their faith. They are known as the Five Ks because each begins with the letter 'K' in the Punjabi language. The Five Ks are *kesh*, uncut hair covered by a turban; *kangha*, a wooden comb which symbolizes cleanliness; *kara*, a steel bracelet symbolizing eternity; *kirpan*, a sword symbolizing strength; and *kaccha*, shorts which symbolize goodness.

Sikh sacred book

The sacred book of the Sikhs is the *Guru Granth Sahib*, or the *Adi Granth*. It is a collection of devotional hymns, composed by six of the gurus and other holy men. They were written down in Gurmukhi, the script used for writing the Punjabi language. Gurmukhi means 'from the Guru's mouth'. Every copy of the *Guru Granth Sahib* has 1,430 pages. When Guru Gobind Singh, the tenth and last Guru, died in 1708, he told the Sikhs that their next Guru would not be a living person but the sacred scripture. In the *gurdwara*, the Sikh community centre, the *Guru Granth Sahib* is wrapped in a silk cloth and placed on a throne to show how important it is.

Sikh worship

Many Sikhs visit a building called a *gurdwara* to meet together and worship. A *gurdwara* can be any place in which there is a copy of the *Guru Granth Sahib*. Worshippers take off their shoes, cover their heads, bow in front of the sacred scripture and leave offerings of money and food in front of it. Then they sit cross-legged on the floor. The service includes hymns, prayers and readings from the *Guru Granth Sahib*. Afterwards, everyone shares a meal called the *langar* which is cooked in the *gurdwara* kitchen. This shows that everyone is equal, a key Sikh belief.

Right: weddings and other celebrations take place in the gurdwara, *in front of the* Guru Granth Sahib.

Map showing Sikh areas of the Indian subcontinent.

Kashmir

Guru Nanak's birthplace — Punjab — Amritsar Temple

Rajasthan — Uttar Pradesh

Gujarat

Mumbai

Calcutta

INDIA

Distribution of the Sikh population.

Priests as healers

In many traditional societies, a type of priest called a shaman, or witch doctor, is believed to have powers of healing. The shaman forms a link between the gods and Earth. If a person is sick, the shaman is called to seek out and defeat the evil spirits that are believed to cause illness. The shaman uses his great knowledge of nature to cure the sick person, using medicines made from local plants, berries and roots. Shamans also watch over the dead and guide the souls of the dead to the spirit world.

Left: statue of an ancient American Moche shaman performing a ritual, curing a sick person or praying over a dead person.

Priests and Priestesses

In many of the world's religions, priests and priestesses play a major role as leaders and teachers. In ancient times, priests were extremely important members of society. In some places, the high priest was the king himself. They were believed to act as go-betweens for the worlds of gods and humans, and therefore to possess special powers. People consulted the priests to discover the will of the gods and to find out what the gods had planned for them. This included predictions for the future which the priests made by consulting the stars and natural omens. Today, priests are generally believed to be the representatives of God, or the gods, on Earth, or to have holy powers. They are authorized to perform religious rituals and ceremonies which ordinary worshippers cannot perform.

Above: a shaman, or witch doctor from Cameroon, Africa.

Priests as teachers

In many religions, priests and priestesses act as teachers, helping people to find out more about their faith. In Judaism, religious teachers are called rabbis. They study the *Torah*, the Jewish holy book, lead worship in the synagogues and conduct weddings and funerals. They also help Jews in their community, giving advice on spiritual issues and visiting the old and sick.

Above: a rabbi reading the Torah, *using a silver pointer, called a* yad.

Right: some of the most important shamans of Guatemala are women.

Invoking the spirits

The shaman is believed to have the power to communicate with the spirit world. In a deep trance, the shaman's soul is believed to visit the spirits to speak to them on a person's behalf. This may be to ask for a cure for a sick person or, in places where people survive by hunting or farming, to ask the spirits to send lots of animals and good weather.

Right: a Thunder Block used by shamans in Hong Kong to ward off evil spirits.

Left: in Fiji, temple priests sipped an intoxicating drink from a small, flat dish like this one to help them go into a trance.

Rituals and offerings

Priests or priestesses receive special training to perform rituals and ceremonies. In many religions it is the priest's duty to make offerings or to lead groups in ritual as intermediaries between worshippers and the gods. For Hindus, the priest alone is allowed into the inner sanctum where the sacred images stand. He takes devotees' offerings and performs *puja* (worship) for them. Then he returns part of the offerings to them, to bestow God's blessings on them.

Left: modern Druid priestesses celebrating the summer solstice in England with rites and rituals. The origins of Druidism date to Celtic times (see pages 12–13).

Right: each Hindu temple has its own priests, or pujaris, *who come from the highest Brahman caste.*

Serving the community

In addition to their religious duties, priests and priestesses have always performed valuable services in their communities. In ancient Rome, the Vestal Virgins, left, were responsible for keeping the sacred fire burning to ensure the safety of Rome. In China, Taoist priests are either monastic, or live at home and perform religious ceremonies and rituals whenever necessary. Their role is to perform the harmonizing rites that will bring the people in their community good health and long life.

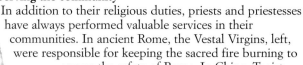
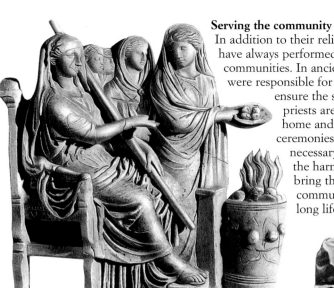

Above: Vestal Virgins attending the sacred fire of ancient Rome.

Left: a Taoist priest from Taiwan in ritual costume.

Spreading God's word

In many religions, priests and teachers help to spread the word of God by preaching sermons and giving talks. In Islam, an *imam* is a religious leader who teaches and leads the mosque community. The *imam* leads prayers in the mosque and gives a talk at Friday prayers. In many Christian churches, the minister or priest preaches a sermon as part of a service. He or she usually takes a passage from the Bible as a theme.

Right: an imam *addressing a congregation from his pulpit in the mosque.*

Left: in Japan, Shinto priests lead rituals performed to ensure the well-being of the community.

Above: this Confucian priest from South Korea, descendant of a royal family, leads a ritual in honour of the ancestors.

Leaders of the church

Some religions have an overall leader or authority. The Pope is head of the Roman Catholic Church. The word pope means 'father'. From his headquarters in the Vatican City, the Pope oversees the Roman Catholic Church across the world. Roman Catholics believe that the Pope takes the place of Jesus's disciple, Peter, who led the first Christians and became the first Bishop of Rome.

Below: a woman minister leading a church service.

Above and left: the scene on this papal throne shows Jesus giving Peter keys to the Kingdom of Heaven.

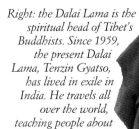

Right: the Dalai Lama is the spiritual head of Tibet's Buddhists. Since 1959, the present Dalai Lama, Tenzin Gyatso, has lived in exile in India. He travels all over the world, teaching people about Buddhism and Tibet.

Women in the church

Traditionally, women have been excluded from many religious activities. During the 20th century, however, some women in the Christian Church have asked to be allowed to become priests and to conduct church services, including Mass or Holy Communion, on an equal footing with men. Many Protestant churches, including the Church of England, have recently allowed women this right.

Chinese Religions

Religious belief in China is made up of many different philosophies and religions. Four of these are particularly important – Taoism, Confucianism, Buddhism and popular, or folk, religion. The first three are known as the *San-chiao*, or the 'three ways'. Chinese people do not feel that they have to choose one religion over the others. They are influenced by all four traditions, and often practise a form of religion that contains elements from each one. The picture on the right shows the founders of the *San-chiao* – Confucius, Lao Tzu, the founder of Taoism, and the Buddha. All three lived at about the same time. While the Buddha was teaching his message in India (see pages 20–21), Confucianism and Taosim were emerging in China. Buddhism came to China in the first century CE and influenced the development of the other two philosophies.

CHINESE RELIGIONS

Origins The teachings of K'ung Fu-tzu or Confucius (551–479 BCE) and Lao-Tzu (6th century BCE) provide the basis for Confucianism and Taoism.

Beliefs Hundreds of gods or immortals and ancestors are worshipped for the well-being of the community.

Adherents Chinese traditional religion: 225 million.

Sacred texts Confucianism: *Five Classics* and the *I-Ching*; Taoism: *Tao Te Ching* and *Chuang-tzu*.

Right: Guan Di, the god of war and protector of the imperial throne.

Map showing:
- Sacred mountain of Taoism
- CHINA
- ZHULU
- ZHAO LU
- LANGYE
- QIN
- Birthplace of Confucius
- HANZHONG
- SHU
- CHU
- WU
- YELLOW SEA
- Birthplace of Lao Tzu

Map showing the cultural areas of ancient China (c. 220 BCE) associated with Taoism and Confucianism.

The Jade Emperor

In Chinese belief, Heaven was divided into different levels. On the top level lived the Jade Emperor, left. He was believed to reside in a luxurious palace and to rule over a court, exactly like that of the emperor on Earth. His courtiers were the souls of nobles and aristocrats, and he had an army of heavenly soldiers. The earthly emperors claimed that Heaven had given them the permission to rule, called the Mandate of Heaven. If the emperor did not rule wisely, Heaven would take the mandate away.

Folk religion

In China, folk religion involves worshipping many different gods and spirits, drawn from myths and legend. These gods and spirits are believed to influence all aspects of nature and daily life and are remembered at colourful festivals, in which the whole community joins. A very important part of folk religion is care of the dead and of ancestors. Elaborate funeral rituals are held to make sure that a dead person's soul reaches Heaven and does not linger as a ghost.

Left: the name of the merciful deity O-mi-t'o Fu is written on stone markers like this one found by the side of a road. These stones are placed in memory of a person who has died prematurely. Each time a passerby reads it he or she is actually saying a prayer for the dead person's soul.

Left: the bodhisattva of compassion, Kuan Yin, of Buddhist origin, is one of the best-loved Chinese goddesses.

Below: the Temple of Heaven in Beijing where the emperor made sacrifices to Heaven.

Taoism

The great Chinese religion of Taoism was founded in the sixth century BCE by a poet and philosopher, Lao Tzu. Not much is known about Lao Tzu's life. According to legend, he tried to leave his home as an old man and ride over the mountains. But the border guard would not let him pass until he had written down his teachings. These poems became the *Tao-te-Ching*, the sacred text of Taoism. Lao Tzu taught that the Tao or 'Way' was the underlying spiritual force of everything in the universe and beyond. The aim of a Taoist was to live in harmony with the Tao, in order to free oneself from the material world, liberate the soul and ultimately gain immortality. To achieve harmony, many Taoists use meditation, chanting and physical exercise such as *T'ai Chi* to bring the body's energy forces into balance.

Below: Lao Tzu, the founder of Taoism, travelling on the back of an ox.

Left: a stone sculpture of Heavenly Worth, another of the Taoist Immortals. He would originally have been flanked by two attendants.

Above: Li T'ieh-kuai, one of the eight Immortals of Taoism, who appears as a beggar with an iron crutch. The Immortals are examples of how everyone can gain immortality. There are many stories about their deeds.

Yin and Yang

In Chinese religion, two opposite but complementary forces, called *yin* and *yang*, are believed to be responsible for all creation. They are represented by the symbol shown in cloth in the painting on the left. Traditionally, *yin* is associated with water, darkness, cold, inactivity and the female. *Yang* is associated with air, light, heat, activity and the male. Each half of the symbol contains the seed or essence of its opposite.

Left: a Taoist judge of Hell who judged the souls of the dead and handed out suitable punishments for their sins.

Confucianism

Along with Taoism and Buddhism, Confucianism is the most important system of beliefs in China. But Confucius did not intend to start a new religion. He gave up his job in the government to teach people how to live in peace and harmony. Confucius believed that the way to achieve this was to respect other people and honour the memory of one's ancestors. Each person's well-being depended on the well-being of others. Confucius taught people five virtues to follow – kindness, wisdom, loyalty, righteousness and sobriety. The sacred texts of Confucianism are called the *Five Classics*. They consist of poems, rituals, history and the wise sayings of Confucius and his followers. So influential were they that they were used to train Chinese civil servants until the early 20th century.

Left: Confucius (c. 551–479 BCE) dedicated his life to finding the best way to live in the world by being wise, kind and dutiful.

Below: Mao Tse-tung (1893–1976), historic leader of China's Communist Party.

Below: one of the main gateways of the Temple of Confucius at Qufu in China.

Religion in the People's Republic

The political changes in China in the 20th century have had a great effect on how people practise their religion. The Communist Party did not approve of religion, even though one of its most important leaders, Mao Tse-tung, was revered almost as much as a god. During the Cultural Revolution in the 1960s and 70s, many temples and monasteries were destroyed, and religious teachers were denounced. Despite this, many people continued to follow their religious beliefs.

Japanese Religions

Religion in Japan is a rich mixture of traditions and beliefs. The ancient religion of Japan is called Shinto, which means 'the way of the *kami*'. It began thousands of years ago in prehistoric Japan. Its followers believe in spirits, called *kami*, which inhabit animals, plants and natural places like mountains, rivers, rocks and trees. Shinto does not have a founder or a supreme power. There is no collection of sacred texts nor a fixed system of beliefs. Many people mix Shinto beliefs with those of Buddhism, Japan's other main religion. It is not unusual, for example, for Japanese people to have a Shinto wedding and a Buddhist funeral. In the 18th and 19th centuries, a movement began to revive classical Shinto in Japan. A system called 'State Shinto' was started in which religion served the government, and the Japanese emperor was worshipped as divine. This system ended in 1945.

Below: a stone statue of a fox, the messenger of the rice god, Inari.

Above: a terracotta figure of an earth goddess believed to be a mythological ancestor from Hokkaido. Figures like this one were made long ago for fertility rites.

The *kami*

According to legend, the *kami* are spirits that came down to Earth to inhabit natural places such as mountains, rivers and rice fields. There are thousands of *kami*, usually divided into heavenly *kami* and earthly *kami*. The most important include the creators, Izanagi and Izanami, Amaterasu and Inari, god of rice. But any places or beings that inspire awe, such as animals, birds, rocks and trees, could be called *kami*. The spirits of extraordinary human beings such as emperors, heroes and great teachers, can also become *kami*.

The creation myth

In Shinto myth, the world was created by the god Izanagi and his wife, Izanami. They stood on the Floating Bridge of Heaven and stirred the water beneath, bringing forth the islands of Japan. Izanagi and Izanami had many children, who became the gods of nature. Then tragedy struck. Izanami died while giving birth to the fire god. Izanagi tried in vain to bring his wife back from the land of the dead, where eight thunder gods guarded her body. Then he plunged into the sea to wash his grief away.

Left: one of the eight thunder gods.

The sun goddess

The most important *kami* is Amaterasu, the sun goddess and daughter of Izanagi and Izanami. Until very recently, she was worshipped as the ancestor of the Japanese imperial family. Amaterasu's main shrine is at Ise. The shrine houses the sacred mirror which the goddess's spirit is said to enter to listen to prayers addressed to her.

Above: a sword, a jewel and a mirror are symbols of the kami. The mirror is particularly powerful since it is associated with the goddess Amaterasu.

Left: Kishijoten, also known as Benten, is the goddess of love.

Right: Fujin, the god of the winds, carrying a sack of winds on his back.

This map shows Japan, the location of Shinto shrines and one of the most sacred mountains, Mt. Fuji.

• *Site of Shinto shrine*

CHINA

HOKKAIDO

JAPAN

SEA OF JAPAN

KOREAN PENINSULA

HONSHU

Tokyo

SHIKOKU Ise

KYUSHU

Mt. Fuji

PACIFIC OCEAN

The seven gods of happiness

The *Shichi Fukujin*, or seven gods of happiness, are believed to bring good fortune to worshippers. They are very popular gods in Shinto worship. Although they are of different Shinto, Buddhist and Hindu origins, they hold an important role in Shinto life, being associated with all aspects of human life, such as long life, love, wealth and work.

Buddhism in Japan

Buddhism reached Japan in the sixth century CE, brought by monks from Korea and China. Many different schools of Buddhism developed, all belonging to the *Mahayana* group (see page 21). Today about three-quarters of Japanese people are Buddhists, although many mix Shinto and Buddhist beliefs. Among the most popular and best-known schools are *Pure Land* and Zen. Followers of *Pure Land* Buddhism worship the *bodhisattva* Amida, lord of a beautiful peaceful place called the *Pure Land*. By praying to him, his followers believe that they will go to the *Pure Land*, closer to *nirvana*, when they die. Zen Buddhism was founded by an Indian monk, Bodhidharma. Its name means 'meditation', and Zen Buddhists use many different meditation techniques to help them gain self-awareness.

Right: statue of Kongo-yasha, a terrible incarnation of the Buddha Fuku. His role is to guard against evil, so he has a terrifying appearance.

Right: Bodhidharma, the Indian monk who founded Zen Buddhism.

Left: Hotei Osho, one of the seven gods of happiness, is a popular form of the bodhisattava Miroku.

Above: a Shinto torii *or gateway.*

Shinto worship

There are thousands of shrines all over Japan where the *kami* are worshipped. Visiting the shrines is a central part of Shinto worship. A baby is carried to a shrine for its first visit when it is only one month old. Worshippers must follow a set of elaborate rituals as they approach the shrine. They enter through a wooden gateway, or *torii* which separates the sacred world of the shrine from the outside world. At the entrance is a water trough where they wash their hands and mouths. Then they proceed to the worship hall, or *haiden*, where they make offerings of money, make two deep bows before the shrine, clap their hands twice and bow again to welcome the *kami*. Then they offer up their prayers. Beyond the *haiden* is the *honden,* or inner shrine, where the *kami* lives. Only priests may enter here.

Right: worshippers visit Shinto shrines to make special requests. On New Year's Day, fuda, or paper amulets, with the name of the shrine or the kami *written on them, are sold at shrine entrances. Worshippers place them in a* butsudan, *or altar, to bring them good luck and protection in the new year.*

Below: worshippers write their prayers or requests on prayer boards, or emas, *and hang them on a wall in the shrine.*

Right: a shrine offering of a paper ornament dangling from a branch.

Left: Children's Day is celebrated in November at the Meiji shrine in Tokyo. Parents take their children along to receive blessings for their futures.

Festivals and celebrations

Many festivals and celebrations are held at Shinto shrines. Each shrine has a yearly festival when people flock to the shrine to worship the *kami* and enjoy themselves. At festival times, a portable shrine, or *mikoshi*, is paraded through the streets so that the whole community can be blessed and protected by the *kami*. Family celebrations, like the wedding shown on the right, also take place in the shrine.

Left: a scene from an ancient Babylonian carving shows the god Shanash giving a code of laws to King Hammurabi.

Right: part of the Egyptian Book of the Dead, a collection of spells and instructions buried in tombs. They were thought to help the dead person's soul on its journey through the afterlife.

Early writings
Since the invention of writing, worshippers have recorded sacred texts to establish laws and rituals. The sacred texts of Hinduism, the *Vedas*, were composed about 3,500 years ago. They were four collections of prayers, hymns and magic spells. For centuries, the texts were handed down by word of mouth. Later, they were written down in Sanskrit, the ancient, sacred language of India. Sanskrit means 'perfected'. It was believed to have special powers for communicating with the gods.

Sacred Texts

Sacred texts, or scriptures, play a central part in many faiths. They tell devotees more about their religion and about what God or the deities wish for the world. Some tell the story of the lives of religious founders and teachers, and contain accounts of their teachings. Some are believed to have been communicated directly from God, and are called revealed scriptures, or *revelations*. Whatever their origins are, sacred texts are treated with great respect and reverence. Many are studied and read as part of worship and in festivals and celebrations. They provide people with guidance about how they should live their lives in the way that God or the deities wish.

Right: the powers of the Vedas were effective only if the priests were word-perfect when reciting from the texts.

Left: a Mayan book, written on a long strip of bark and folded into pages. The texts were guides for priests telling them how to carry out rituals correctly.

Below: an exquisite keter, or crown, placed on top of the Torah scrolls in a synagogue.

Above: a special container in the shape of a mosque for keeping a copy of the Qur'an.

Teachings of the texts
Many scriptures contain the key teachings of a particular faith. The illustration of Mahavira, above, is a page from the *Kalpa Sutra*, one of the most sacred texts of the Jains. Dating from the first century BCE, it is an account of Mahavira's life, together with details of rituals.

Illuminated manuscripts

Until the invention of printing, every book had to be copied and illustrated by hand. Because each book took many months to produce, few were made and they were very expensive. Artists developed special techniques for decorating religious manuscripts. In the Middle Ages, each Christian monastery had its own *scriptorium*, a room where monks produced copies of sacred texts. These manuscripts were works of art, beautifully decorated with drawings and 'illuminated' letters, coloured with bright reds, blues, greens and precious gold leaf.

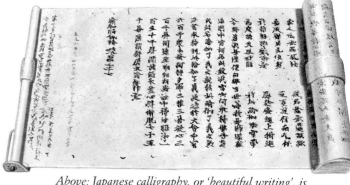

Above: Japanese calligraphy, or 'beautiful writing', is used to reflect the spirit of this Zen Buddhist manuscript. Master calligraphers are highly respected for their work.

Above: the cover of a medieval Bible with the figure of Jesus surrounded by the symbols of the four Evangelists.

Above: this silver fish contains a Jewish Purim scroll with the Book of Esther. It is read on the feast day of Purim.

Right: a beautifully decorated page from a Qur'an.

Translating the sacred texts

As religions spread, translations were made of their sacred texts. Christian texts have been translated all over the world in many different languages. The text on the left is a *Gadl*, an account of the lives of the Christian saints, from Ethiopia. The *Qur'an*, right, is the sacred book of Islam. Muslims always study the *Qur'an* in its original Arabic because this was the language in which it was revealed. Any translation is thought to lose some of its meaning and spirit.

Above: a Gadl written on goatskin or sheepskin.

Below: in Buddhism, monks who undertook the task of translating the sacred texts were greatly honoured.

Right: this illustration shows Gutenberg standing before his press holding a printed book.

Printing sacred texts

In about 1438, a German craftsman, Johannes Gutenberg invented the first printing press. It pressed a sheet of paper onto a tray of inked metal letters to print a page. In 1455, Gutenberg produced the world's first printed Bible. The Bible was in two volumes of 600 pages each. The colours and illustrations were added later by hand. Gutenberg printed about 160 copies. Today, modern printing presses mean that millions of books can be printed and distributed all over the world.

Preserving sacred texts

After the Chinese occupied Tibet in 1950, many monastery libraries were ransacked and priceless Buddhist manuscripts were destroyed. Despite the difficulties, copying and caring for the scriptures continues. These monks are cleaning and checking the 108 volumes of the *Kanjur*, the Tibetan translation of the Buddhist canon. The books are written on long, rectangular pages, bound between wood. The shape of the pages mimics the long, narrow palm leaves on which the scriptures were first written.

The Origins of Judaism

Judaism is the world's oldest monotheistic religion, that is, the first of the great faiths to believe in just one God. The history of Judaism goes back about 4,000 years to the time when the Jews were a nomadic people called the Hebrews who lived in the Middle East. A man called Abraham is believed to have been the first Jew and Judaism's founding father. The scriptures say that Abraham entered into a covenant or agreement with God. God promised Abraham that he would make him the father of a great nation if he obeyed him and taught his laws to the world. To mark the covenant, Abraham was circumcised, as is the practice for all Jewish men today.

Below: Abraham, following God's word, led his people out of Mesopotamia.

Kingdom of Israel and Judah
Vassal kingdoms
● *Site of building project in reign of Solomon*
— *Boundary of Solomon's Empire*

ARAM (SYRIA)

● **Hazor**

GESHUR

● **Megiddo**

ISRAEL

AMMON

Gezer ●

Baalath ●　● **Bethhoron**

Jerusalem ●

PHILISTIA

JUDAH

MOAB

Tamar ● *This map shows...*

EDOM

Map showing Israelite territories during Solomon's reign (c. 965–928 BCE).

Origins

At the time Judaism began, people in Abraham's homeland of Mesopotamia worshipped many different gods. They included the mother goddess, left. Unhappy with this, Abraham began to worship one God instead. The Hebrew Bible tells how he responded to God's call to leave home and follow him.

Above: a terracotta figure of a Mesopotamian goddess.

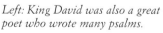

Left: Moses holding up the Ten Commandments.

Jewish leaders

In the Jewish tradition, Abraham was the first of three men called the patriarchs, or fathers, of Judaism. The other two were his son, Isaac, and his grandson, Jacob. Centuries after Abraham, another great leader emerged. Moses led the Jews out of slavery in Egypt and on their long journey to the promised land of Israel. The Jews believe that it was through Moses that God gave them the books of the *Torah*. Moses climbed Mount Sinai to hear the *Torah* and bring the Ten Commandments back to the people (see page 44).

Right: Isaiah was an important prophet, a writer or teacher inspired by God. His teachings gave his people hope during their exile in Babylon.

Left: King David was also a great poet who wrote many psalms.

Below: a gate from the royal centre of Hazor built during the rein of Solomon.

Right: the Book of Genesis tells how the Tower of Babel was built in Babylon, in an attempt to reach Heaven.

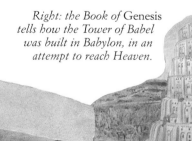

The Age of Kings

After 40 years of wandering in the desert, the Jews reached the Promised Land. At first, they were ruled by leaders called judges. But when the last judge, Samuel, grew old, the Jews looked for a king to govern them and establish God's kingdom. The first king of Israel was Saul. He was succeeded by David who, as a young boy, killed the giant Goliath, the champion of the Philistines. David united the kingdom and established his capital city at Jerusalem in 993 BCE. David's son, Solomon, built a magnificent Temple in the city. This became the main centre for Jewish worship.

Exile in Babylon

After King Solomon's death, the kingdom split in two – Israel in the north and Judah in the south. In 587 BCE, Judah was overrun by the Babylonians and Solomon's Temple was destroyed. Many Jews were exiled to Babylon. In Babylon the exiles were free to practise their own religion and form their own communities.

Left: a painting showing the Jews returning to Jerusalem from Babylon.

Right: a reconstruction of the Temple renovated by Herod, ruler of the Jews from 37 to 4 BCE.

Many invaders

In 333 BCE, the Persian Empire was overthrown by Alexander the Great. He and his successors promoted Greek culture, which was fiercely resisted by a section of the Jewish community because it threatened to destroy Jewish identity. In 165 BCE, Judas Maccabaeus led a revolt against the Greek ruler, Antiochus IV, who banned Jewish practices in the Temple. The Temple was rededicated three years later, an event remembered each year at the festival of Hanukkah. By the first century BCE, Israel had come under Roman rule. In 70 CE, in response to a Jewish rebellion, the Romans destroyed Jerusalem and the Second Temple.

Return to Jerusalem

The Jewish exile in Babylon ended in 539 BCE, when the Babylonian Empire was defeated by Cyrus the Great, king of the Persians. The Jews returned in stages. The first large party of exiles found the city in ruins. King Cyrus gave them back all the gold and silver objects which the Babylonians had taken from Solomon's Temple and commanded them to build a new Temple. This was completed in 515 BCE. Another wave of Jews returned from Babylon in 458 BCE.

Left: A limestone altar from the time of the Second Temple.

Right: a detail from a painting showing the destruction of the Temple by the Romans.

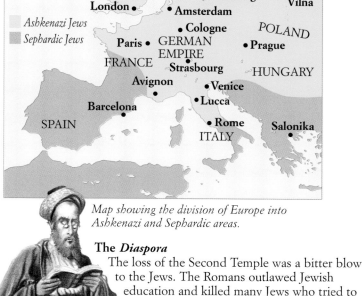

Map showing the division of Europe into Ashkenazi and Sephardic areas.

Ashkenazi Jews
Sephardic Jews

Riga
ENGLAND
London • Hamburg
Vilna
• Amsterdam
• Cologne
POLAND
Paris • GERMAN
EMPIRE • Prague
FRANCE Strasbourg
Avignon HUNGARY
• Venice
Barcelona • Lucca
SPAIN • Rome Salonika
ITALY

Above: this detail from a French Mass book from the 13th century has figures representing the Catholic Church and the Synagogue.

Jews in medieval Europe

In the centuries following the *Diaspora*, the Jews settled in many different countries where they frequently suffered from prejudice and persecution. Their beliefs and customs were mistrusted and used against them. Christian countries were often the worst places for Jews to live. Many were killed or had their belongings confiscated. Others were forced to convert to Christianity or leave the country. In the Middle Ages, thousands of Jews were expelled from England, France and Spain.

The *Diaspora*

The loss of the Second Temple was a bitter blow to the Jews. The Romans outlawed Jewish education and killed many Jews who tried to teach. Many Jews fled from their homeland and spread all over Europe. This became known as the *Diaspora*, or scattering. Two distinct Jewish traditions developed – the *Sephardic* Jews of the Mediterranean (Spain and Portugal), and the *Ashkenazi* Jews of Germany and central Europe.

Right: making a seven-branched candlestick called a menorah, *an important Jewish symbol.*

Above: Ashkenazi Jews from Istanbul from a 19th century illustration.

Right: Jewish communities formed all over the world. This girl is in the traditional costume of Georgia which, although remote from other Jewish communities, adopted Sephardic prayers and laws.

Jewish Life

Today there are about 14 million Jews. They live all over the world, with heavier concentrations in Israel, Europe and the United States. According to Jewish law, anyone who is born of a Jewish mother counts as a Jew whether or not they actively follow Judaism as their religion. Many Jews do not follow any religious practices or beliefs. The basic belief of the Jews is in the existence of one God who created the world and is eternal and invisible. They believe that they have a special relationship with God which dates back to the time of Abraham. They must love God and respect all people. Another important teaching is that, one day, God will send a leader, called the *Messiah*, who will bring peace and harmony for the whole world.

Left: the Star of David, an important Jewish symbol. It dates back to the Middle Ages but is used today on the national flag for the state of Israel.

The Synagogue
The place where Jews can go to worship is called the synagogue. The word synagogue means a meeting place. Synagogues are not only centres for worship, but for study, celebrations and the community. Worship consists of readings from the *Torah* and prayers, often led by a teacher, called a rabbi (see page 26). The holiest part of the synagogue is the Holy Ark, where the sacred *Torah* scrolls are kept.

Living by the word
The Jewish scriptures are called the *Tenakh*, or the Hebrew Bible. It is divided into three parts – the *Torah* (Books of Teaching); the *Nevi'im* (Books of the Prophets); and the *Ketuvim* (Books of Writings). For Jews, the *Torah* is the most important part of their scriptures. These are the teachings which God gave to Moses on Mount Sinai. Jews use the *Torah* as a guide in their daily lives. Copies of the *Torah* are handwritten on scrolls and kept in the synagogue.

Above: the Torah scroll is too sacred to be touched by hands so a pointer, called a yad, *is used instead.*

Above: strict Jews follow a set of rules, found in the Torah, *about food. The rules regulate meals, the preparation of food and the cleaning of utensils and plates. This seal shows that an item is* kosher, *meaning it is clean to use.*

Stages of life
Important events in Jewish life are marked by special ceremonies. Each rite of passage, from the blessing of a baby to remembering the dead, has its own commandments, or *mitzvoth*, which remind people of their duties to God. When a baby boy is born, he is circumcised (the foreskin is removed from his penis) as a sign of the covenant between God and the Jewish people. At 13, a boy has a *Bar Mitzvah* ceremony to mark his entry into adulthood. In the synagogue, he reads from the *Torah* for the first time. When girls reach the age of 12 they celebrate a *Bat Mitzvah*. These ceremonies mark the beginning of adulthood.

Left: a Jewish boy celebrating at his Bar Mitzvah.

Above: instruments used for circumcision.

Right: this 15th century wedding chest is decorated with scenes of a woman following the mitzvoth. *Mitzvoth* are laws which regulate all aspects of Jewish life including marriage and the raising of a family.

Above: the festival of Sukkot takes place in the autumn. It celebrates how the early Jews built shelters in the desert after their escape from Egypt. Palm, willow, myrtle and citron are four plants used as symbols at the festival.

Left: the cup of the prophet Elijah used at the Seder, a meal eaten at Pesach. A place is set at the table for Elijah and his cup is filled with wine but not drunk.

Feast days

The *Shabbat* (Sabbath) is the Jewish holy day. It begins at sunset on Friday and lasts until dusk on Saturday. It is a day for rest and prayer when no work should be done. In Jewish homes, candles are lit and the whole family gathers for a *Shabbat* meal, with readings, prayers and songs. Many Jews visit the synagogue during *Shabbat*. The most important festivals in the Jewish year commemorate key events in Jewish history. *Pesach*, or Passover, in March or April, celebrates the Exodus of the Jews from Egypt. Shavuot celebrates the giving of the *Torah*. *Yom Kippur*, or the Day of Atonement, is the holiest day in the Jewish year. It is a day of prayer and fasting when Jews ask for forgiveness for any wrong they have done.

Left: the festival of Rosh Hashanah celebrates the Jewish New Year. An instrument called a shofar *is blown to wake people to live better lives.*

Above: this calendar counts the days between the feasts of Pesach and Shavuot. This period, called Omer, which lasts for 49 days, is a time of mourning and spiritual purification.

Above: a plate for Purim, the festival which celebrates the story of Esther, a Jewish queen who saved the Jews from tyranny in Persia.

Jewish languages

Many Jews learn to read ancient Hebrew, the language of the *Torah*. Hebrew died out as a spoken language but was revived and is now the official language of Israel. Another Jewish language is Yiddish, a mixture of ancient Hebrew and German. The writing on the cover of this children's book, right, is in Yiddish.

The founding of Israel

In 1948, the state of Israel was founded in Palestine, in the ancient Jewish homeland. It was intended as a safe haven for displaced and persecuted Jews everywhere. Under a law called The Right to Return, Jews from all over the world can claim Israeli citizenship. Many have chosen to live in Israel, inevitably leading to conflict with the Palestinian people (who are mainly Arab Muslims) and the neighbouring Arab states.

Branches of Judaism

There are many different groups of Jews, with different ways of practising their religion. The main groups are Orthodox, Reform and Conservative. Orthodox Jews follow the *Torah* exactly and believe that it must be obeyed without question. In the synagogue, prayers are said in Hebrew, and men and women sit separately. Many Orthodox men wear a *yarmulke* (a round cap for the skull) at all times as a sign of God's presence. Reform and Conservative Jews believe that the *Torah* and religious practice can be adapted to modern life. Everyone sits together in the synagogue, and local languages are used for prayers.

Right: planting of the Israeli flag.

Left: ultra-Orthodox Hasidic Jews. Men wear black hats, suits and white shirts and have beards and side curls.

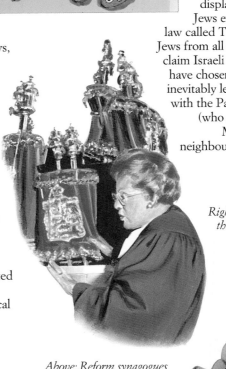

Above: Reform synagogues sometimes have women rabbis who teach and conduct services.

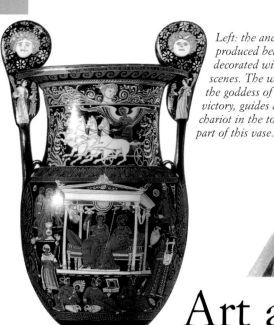

Left: the ancient Greeks produced beautiful vases decorated with mythological scenes. The winged Nike, the goddess of victory, guides a chariot in the top part of this vase.

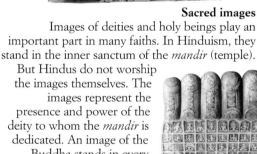

Left: a sacred painting of the Buddha. Ancient rules govern which shapes, patterns and colours artists can use.

Below: the Sri Meenakshi Temple in Madurai, India, is covered with colourful images of gods, goddesses and mythological figures.

Art and Religion

From the earliest times, people have used art to express their religious beliefs, hopes and fears. Prehistoric people painted pictures of the animals they hunted on cave walls. These may have formed part of a religious or magical ritual to ensure better hunting. Since then, religion has inspired some of the greatest works of art, from sacred paintings and images, to vast cathedrals and exquisite mosques. Art has been used to express people's feelings of joy and wonder, to glorify God and to create sacred places of peace and beauty where people can go to worship. Often painting and sculpture are used as symbols, with different colours and shapes having special meanings. This helps to inform worshippers about their faith and illustrates difficult messages which may be hard to understand in words. Aside from its symbolic purpose, religious art has a more practical role. It is also used in a factual way, to record events in a religion's history and in the lives of its founders or leaders.

Sacred artifacts

Many religious artifacts are used as part of worship. They help to remind worshippers of their religion and to focus their minds for meditation. Objects such as reliquaries contain relics such as bones, or something that belonged to a holy person, like clothing. These objects are considered sacred and are venerated. For some they symbolize the presence of the holy person and have the power to work miracles. Many worshippers make pilgrimages (see pages 44–45) to pray for special blessings in the presence of relics. Reliquaries are often made out of precious materials such as gold and gems.

Above: a Buddhist reliquary from Afghanistan.

Above: this page shows the angel Jibril bringing the words of the Qur'an to Muhammad. Most Islamic art, however, does not show people and animals.

Sacred images

Images of deities and holy beings play an important part in many faiths. In Hinduism, they stand in the inner sanctum of the *mandir* (temple). But Hindus do not worship the images themselves. The images represent the presence and power of the deity to whom the *mandir* is dedicated. An image of the Buddha stands in every Buddhist shrine. In early Buddhist art, however, the Buddha was never shown in person but by a symbol, such as a footprint, right.

Sacred images at home

In many religions, people have a small shrine at home where they perform their daily worship. It may contain images of a deity, either in the form of sculptures or paintings. At Chinese New Year, paper pictures of Tsao Chun, the kitchen god, are bought and pasted above the kitchen oven. He reports the family's good and bad deeds to the Jade Emperor in Heaven. Just before New Year, honey is smeared on his mouth to sweeten the words. Then the picture is burned to dispatch Tsao Chun to Heaven.

Left: a statue of Tsao Chun, the kitchen god.

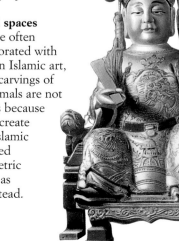

Below: beautiful geometric patterns decorate the wall above the West Gate of the Great Mosque of Cordoba, in Spain.

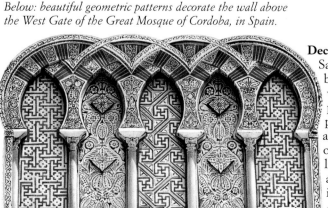

Decorating sacred spaces

Sacred places are often beautifully decorated with works of art. In Islamic art, paintings and carvings of people and animals are not allowed. This is because only Allah can create living things. Islamic artists developed intricate geometric designs to use as decoration instead.

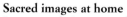
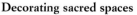

Destruction of images

In times of conflict between two religions, or between a religion and the state, sacred buildings and works of art are often destroyed or badly damaged. In the 16th century, the Christian reformer John Calvin decreed that works of art, such as statues of saints and stained-glass windows, that decorated many churches were signs of frivolity and worldly wealth. He believed that they distracted people's attention away from worshipping God. In some countries, gangs raided churches, smashed windows and burned statues and paintings. Today, many Protestant Christian churches are plain and simple, but many Catholic churches are richly decorated.

Left: a 16th-century statue of the Madonna and Child, a popular theme in Renaissance art. Many similar statues were destroyed.

Art for the afterlife

In many ancient cultures, people were buried with their personal possessions and any other objects they might need in the afterlife. These were intended to help the dead person's soul survive into the next world, and to keep it supplied with food, drink and other necessities. The ancient Egyptians believed that if a dead person's body was not preserved, that person could not attain an afterlife. Therefore, priests performed special ceremonies to preserve the body, and tomb walls of kings and queens were richly decorated with paintings and prayers. Teams of artists created coffins and portrait funeral masks like the one shown on the left.

Left: the Baoulè people of West Africa believe that when people are born they are separated from their spouses from the otherworld and are later reunited with them after death. In times of trouble, figures that represent these spiritual spouses are made so one can feel close to his or her spouse of the spirit world.

Right: kings in ancient China were buried in suits made of jade, a precious stone. A symbol of immortality, jade was believed to provide a connection between Heaven and Earth.

Left: traditional Hawaiian chants in honour of the gods are considered a sacred language. Trained dancers accompany the chants, telling stories with movements of the body while following the beat of a ceremonial drum.

Telling stories

Many different art forms, including painting and the performing arts, like music and dance, are used to communicate and pass down myths or stories from one generation to the next. For centuries, the Australian Aborigines have recorded their myths and stories with paintings. Some Aborigine art dates back more than 30,000 years. Scenes from the Dreaming, a time long ago when the spirits of the ancestors roamed the land and shaped the landscape, were painted on rocks, on the ground, on bark and on people's bodies.

Influence of other cultures

In some examples of religious art, two styles have mixed to create a new style. This happened in the 13th century in Spain which was influenced both by Western Christian and Eastern Islamic culture. Colours used by Christian artists were combined with Islamic design to create exquisite works of art.

Left: this illustration was used in a biblical manuscript copied in Spain in 1260. The central decoration is Islamic in style but the colours are Western.

The Origins of Christianity

Christians follow the teachings of a man called Jesus Christ who lived about 2,000 years ago in Palestine. His life, death and resurrection form the basis of the Christian faith. Today most of Palestine is known as Israel. In Jesus's time, it was a mostly Jewish country, ruled by the Romans. Jesus himself was born and raised as a Jew, and gained many followers among ordinary Jewish people. The religious authorities, however, were suspicious of his revolutionary teachings, and plotted his capture and death. In the centuries after Jesus's death, his followers spread his teachings all over the world.

Below: Mary, Joseph and the infant Jesus, in the manger where he was born.

The birth of Jesus

According to the Christian Bible, God sent the angel Gabriel, above, to announce to Mary that she would become Jesus's mother. Jesus was born in Bethlehem where Mary and her husband, Joseph, had gone to take part in a census. The town was crowded and there was nowhere to stay, so Jesus was born in a humble stable. The Bible tells how shepherds and wise men came to visit the newborn baby. Jesus was brought up in Nazareth, his parents' hometown, and was probably trained to be a carpenter, like his father.

Parables and miracles

In his teaching, Jesus often used simple stories, called parables, to get difficult messages across. Each parable had a spiritual lesson to teach. The parable of the Good Samaritan, for example, tells the story of how a traveller is helped by a man traditionally considered an enemy. Jesus also gained a reputation for performing miracles. These were not magic tricks but signs of God's spiritual power.

Left: Jesus restores a blind man's sight.

Below: Jesus and some of his disciples.

This map shows some of the journeys Jesus made and the places he visited.

Ministry and disciples

When Jesus was about 30 years old, he asked his cousin, John, to baptize him in the River Jordan. This was a sign of washing away sin and starting a new life. For the next three years, Jesus travelled the region, teaching and preaching. He spoke of God as a loving father and told people to repent of their sins and to love and care for others. Jesus chose 12 men to be his closest companions, or his disciples.

Death and resurrection

In the last week of his life, Jesus went to Jerusalem for the Passover festival. He was arrested and charged with blasphemy (taking God's name in vain). The Roman governor, Pontius Pilate, sentenced Jesus to death and he was crucified on a cross. His body was later taken down and buried in a tomb. Three days later, the tomb was empty – Jesus had risen from the dead. The scriptures say that he appeared to his disciples several times before ascending to Heaven to be with God.

Above: a scene showing Jesus's crucifixion, from an Ethiopian manuscript.

Below: an angel tells Jesus's friends that he has risen from the dead and shows them his empty tomb.

The early Church

After his death, Jesus's followers spread the Christian faith all over the known world. Tradition says that Saint Peter, the leader of the disciples, travelled to Rome where he died a martyr during the persecution of the Christians. He was later named as the first Bishop of Rome, or Pope. One of the greatest early Christian leaders was Saint Paul. Formerly a strict Jew called Saul, he had a vision of Jesus that changed his life. Filled with a new faith in Christ, he began to preach. Paul travelled throughout the Roman Empire, setting up Christian communities and teaching people about Jesus. His letters, or epistles, gave encouragement and advice to the early Christians who were a minority group in the Roman Empire. In 313 CE, however, the Roman emperor Constantine, made Christianity the official religion and persecution ended.

Above: Saints Peter and Paul.

Above: the Roman emperor, Constantine.

The writing of the Gospels

The Gospels were written roughly 50 years after Jesus's death by the four Evangelists, Matthew, Mark, Luke and John. They are accounts of Jesus's life and teachings, written with the intention of converting people to Christianity. The Gospels (meaning 'good news') are found in the New Testament of the Bible, the Christians' sacred book. The other part of the Bible is the Old Testament, which contains the ancient Jewish scriptures. The Bible is the basis of Christian teaching, revealing God's will and giving Christians a guide for living. Many Christians read the Bible for daily worship.

Left: St. Mark was traditionally symbolized as a lion. The other Evangelists are symbolized by a man (Matthew), an ox (Luke) and an eagle (John).

Left: Charlemagne was crowned ruler of the Holy Roman Empire by the Pope in 800 CE.

The Great Schism

In the fifth century, the Roman Empire split into two. The city of Constantinople became the capital of the Eastern or Byzantine Empire, while Rome remained the capital of the Western Empire. In 1054, a dispute arose between the heads of the Church in Constantinople and Rome. This led to a major split, called the Great Schism, between the two branches of the Church and it was firmly divided into eastern and western branches. The Western Church became known as the Roman Catholic Church, based on the authority of the Pope. The eastern part became known as the Orthodox Church.

Map showing main religious beliefs in Europe c. 1050 CE.

The Holy Roman Empire

In the Middle Ages, the Popes, or Bishops of Rome, grew in importance. In 800 CE, Pope Leo III crowned Charlemagne ruler of the Holy Roman Empire, an action which symbolized the special role of the papacy at the head of the Christian Church. Charlemagne was born in 742 CE. He led his armies out of France and conquered large parts of Europe. A Christian, Charlemagne forced non-believers, such as the Saxons, to convert to Christianity and take part in mass baptisms. Charlemagne was regarded by many as the ideal ruler, and the empire he founded lasted in one form or another until 1806.

RUSSIA

EMPIRE OF GERMANY

Vladimir • • Kiev • *KHAZAR KHANATE*

• Prague

Venice • • Belgrade • Cherson

Rome • • Sofia

Thessalonica • Constantinople

Mt. Athos • *BYZANTINE EMPIRE* • Antioch

Athens

Jerusalem •

Alexandria •

☐ Roman Catholic Church
☐ Orthodox Church
☐ Area of mixed influence
☐ Islam

Left: a reliquary of the holy cross, a symbol of Christ's crucifixion.

Right: a replica in the form of the Church of the Holy Sepulcher in Jerusalem, commissioned for Tsar Ivan III in 1486 for the Kremlin Cathedral.

The Eastern Church

The influence of the Eastern, or Orthodox, Church spread to Eastern Europe, Greece and Russia. Each branch has its own customs and language but they all share the same ancient traditions of worship. Orthodox churches are often very lavish, and richly decorated with holy pictures called icons. These pictures of saints, angels and other holy figures are used as a focus for worship.

The Crusades

In the 11th century, Christian forces from Europe began a series of religious and military expeditions known as the Crusades. Their aim was to conquer the Holy Land and free Jerusalem from the Muslim Turks who ruled Palestine at that time. In 1095, the Muslims banned Christian pilgrims from visiting Jerusalem and its holy sites. This led to the launching of the First Crusade in 1096. In three years, the Crusaders had defeated the Muslims and captured Jerusalem. None of the seven later Crusades matched this success, however, and Jerusalem was eventually retaken by the Muslims.

Right: three holy fathers of the Eastern Orthodox Church, from a 15th-century Russian icon.

The World of Christianity

CHRISTIANITY

Origins Christianity was founded by Jesus Christ in modern-day Israel during the first century CE.

Beliefs There are three beings in one God (the Father, the Son and the Holy Spirit) who is merciful and forgiving. Christians follow the teachings of Jesus Christ, the son of God.

Main subdivisions Roman Catholic, Orthodox and Protestant.

Adherents about 2 billion.

Sacred texts Bible (including the Old and New Testament).

There are many different groups of Christians around the world. They vary in their customs and worship but share the same basic beliefs. Christians believe that Jesus was the Christ, or 'anointed one', who came to save the world from sin by giving up his own life. Although he lived on Earth as a human, they believe that he was the Son of God and, therefore, divine. Christians worship one God who they believe is infinite and eternal. They think of God as a loving father who cares for people as if they were his children. God is referred to in three ways, known as the Trinity – God the Father (the creator of the world), God the Son (Jesus Christ) and God the Holy Spirit (God's presence in the world). These are not three separate beings, but three beings combined in one God.

Above: Martin Luther preaching.

Veneration of saints

Some Christians, such as the Roman Catholic and the Orthodox, honour many saints. Saints are people who have led holy lives and who, after their deaths, are able to help worshippers in need through their intercession.

Left: a 15th century stained-glass window depicting Mary with the infant Jesus. Many special feast days are celebrated in her honour.

Right: the title page of a book defending the Catholic Church that belonged to King Henry VIII of England, who broke away from the Church, establishing the Anglican Church.

The Reformation

In the 16th century, a German monk, Martin Luther (1483–1546), protested that the Catholic Church had become too rich, powerful and corrupt, and called for reform. He attacked the authority of the Pope, and, in particular, condemned the sale of indulgences, the Church custom of taking money from people in return for pardoning them for their sins. Luther also translated the Bible into German. Until then, it had only been read in Latin, which ordinary people could not understand. His ideas began a movement called the Reformation which led to the founding of the Protestant Church.

Christian worship

Christians worship God privately with prayers at home, or publicly by joining others in a church. Sunday is a special day to be reserved for worship. Most church services are conducted by a priest or minister, who also delivers a sermon or talk. They include singing hymns, saying prayers and listening to Bible readings. For Christians, the most important ritual is the Eucharist, when the congregation shares bread and wine. Also known as Mass or Communion, it commemorates the Last Supper when Jesus shared bread and wine with his disciples, saying that the bread was his body and the wine his blood.

Left: by sharing bread and wine, Christians remember Jesus's death and resurrection.

Left: special stamps found in the Roman catacombs for stamping Communion bread.

The sacraments

The spiritual life of a Christian is marked by different stages called sacraments. The sacraments are special blessings usually received during ritual ceremonies conducted by a priest or minister. Baptism and the Eucharist (see above) are two of the most important sacraments that are shared by all Christians. Baptism, the first sacrament, signifies the beginning of Christian life. Not all Christians, however, share the same sacraments. Holy Matrimony, or marriage, is a sacrament which is celebrated when a couple decides to live together and begin a family of their own.

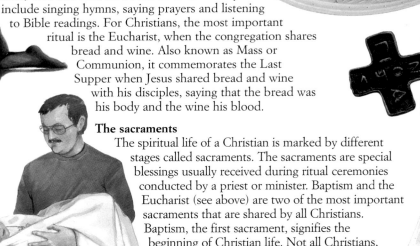

Above: baptism is a sacrament which often takes place soon after a child is born. The priest makes the sign of the cross in water on the baby's forehead to welcome him or her into the Church. Some Christians believe in adult baptism.

Right: during the celebration of holy matrimony the exchange of rings is symbolic of the vows a couple makes before God and the Christian community.

Religious life

Some Christians feel called to live as monks or nuns. They live in monasteries or convents and devote their lives to God, taking three vows – of poverty, chastity and obedience. Among the best-known groups, or orders, are the Cistercians, Dominicans, Franciscans and Benedictines. Some cut themselves off from the outside world, to concentrate on reflection and prayer. Others play an important part in local communities by teaching and working with local people. Some Christians train to become priests or ministers. After several years of study, they become leaders of parishes, where they look after their parishioners' needs.

Above: a Cistercian monk.

Below: a painting by a 17th-century Mughal artist showing mass being celebrated in India.

Below: Nuns accepting a novice into their community.

Right: a scene showing Jesus's birth, or Nativity. Tradition says that three wise men visited Jesus and brought him precious gifts of gold, frankincense and myrrh. The festival of Epiphany on January 6 celebrates their arrival.

Feast days

The most important festivals in the Christian year celebrate events in Jesus's life. Christmas commemorates Jesus's birth in Bethlehem about 2,000 years ago. Preparations begin on the fourth Sunday before Christmas Day, which marks the beginning of Advent which means 'coming'. Christmas Day is traditionally celebrated on December 25 (January 6 in the Orthodox Church). At Christmas, people decorate their homes, and exchange gifts and cards to celebrate this joyful time. Easter is the most important festival in the Christian calendar. On Good Friday, Christians remember the day on which Jesus died on the cross. This is a time for prayer and contemplation. Easter Sunday is a joyful time, when Jesus is believed to have risen from the dead.

Left: the week before Easter is called Holy Week. It begins with Palm Sunday, when Jesus rode into Jerusalem. On Maundy Thursday, Jesus ate the Last Supper with his disciples. As a sign of humility, Jesus washed his disciples' feet.

The spread of Christianity

From its origins in the Middle East, Christianity has spread all over the world. Today, it is the world's largest religion, practised in almost every country by about two billion followers. The first missionaries were Jesus's own disciples, and other leaders, such as Saint Paul. From the 14th century, European explorers from the great empires of Spain, Portugal and Britain claimed the new lands they discovered in the name of God and started converting the local people to Christianity, often by force. Missionary work continues today, in Africa, India and South-east Asia.

Right: the early Christians adopted the lamb with a cross as a symbol of the sacrifice Jesus made when he died on the cross. It is also a symbol of Jesus's resurrection.

Right: in 1950 Mother Teresa of Calcutta founded the Order of Missionaries of Charity, a group of Roman Catholic women dedicated to helping the poor and the sick. Today, even after Mother Teresa's death in 1997, the order continues to work, providing aid to those in need.

Local worship

Missionary groups have travelled to Asia and Africa to spread their beliefs and provide assistance to the poor. In some countries to which Christianity has spread, missionaries have upset local people by imposing their views and not respecting the local culture and traditions. In some places, however, local beliefs continue to exist side by side with Christianity, and people have found ways to worship by combining the two.

Left: Christian communities all over the world have their own ways of worshipping, like this group from Africa.

Holy Places

In each of the world's religions, certain places are considered sacred. Every year, millions of devotees make journeys, called pilgrimages, to these holy sites. There are many reasons why people feel that it is important to make a pilgrimage. They may want to pray for something special, like good health, to remember a loved one or important event, or to give thanks for a wish that has come true. Some places of pilgrimage are believed to have healing powers or to wash away people's sins. For many people, however, a pilgrimage is an act of worship in itself, a way of feeling closer to God.

Left: for Jews, Christians and Muslims, Mount Sinai is where God revealed himself to Moses. God told Moses to remove his shoes because he was standing on holy ground.

Below: some Native Americans marked a sacred place with a painted buffalo skull.

Sacred ground

Sites of pilgrimage may be buildings, such as temples or tombs, or natural places, such as rivers or mountains. Reaching them often involves a long and difficult journey, an act of merit in itself. In many religions, mountains are thought to be sacred, as meeting places between Heaven and Earth. Mount Fuji in Japan is sacred to followers of Shinto. It is considered the home of the gods. Thousands of pilgrims climb the mountain each year to visit its numerous shrines.

Above: a painting of the goddess Amaterasu appearing above Mount Fuji.

Left: the Parthenon in Athens, which stands on the Acropolis, the highest point of the city, was the main temple of the Greek goddess Athena, patron goddess of the city. The ancient Greeks believed that the gods were present on the Acropolis.

Below: the Vatican City in Rome, Italy is an important pilgrimage site for Roman Catholics. Pilgrims from all over the world visit the tomb of St. Peter, their first leader, in St. Peter's Cathedral. Today the Vatican City is home to St. Peter's successor, the Pope.

Ancient places of worship

Ancient people had their own sacred places where they practised their religious rites and rituals. Some of these still stand today. The stone circle of Stonehenge stands in the middle of Salisbury Plain in England. Dating from about 3,000 BCE, it may have been built as an ancient temple to the sun or as a giant calendar used to plot the position of the sun and stars, and to calculate the length of the year.

Right: the ancient stone circle of Stonehenge is particularly revered by modern Druids.

The Holy Land

The lands of Israel and Palestine are sacred to Jews, Christians and Muslims. For Jews, it is the region promised to them by God. Moses led their ancestors to the Promised Land after they escaped from their exile in Egypt. For Christians, the Holy Land is the place where Jesus was born, taught and died. The picture above, from an 18th-century illustration, shows the Temple Mount in Jerusalem, the Jews' holiest site. Pictured in the centre is the Islamic Dome of the Rock. Muslims believe that this is the place from which the Prophet Muhammad made his journey into Heaven.

Below: a cross-section of the Church of the Holy Sepulcher in Jerusalem. It is thought to stand on the site where Jesus was crucified, buried and where he rose from the dead.

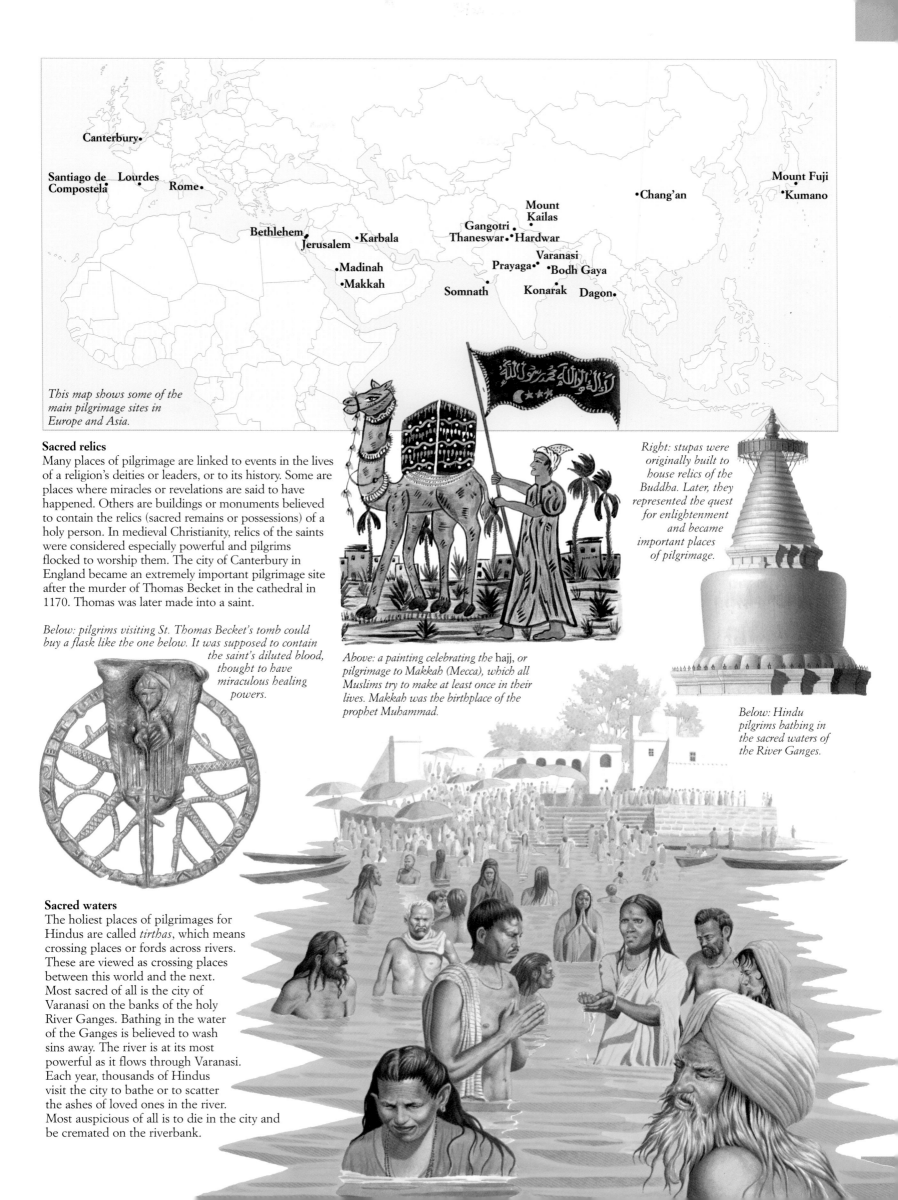

This map shows some of the main pilgrimage sites in Europe and Asia.

Sacred relics

Many places of pilgrimage are linked to events in the lives of a religion's deities or leaders, or to its history. Some are places where miracles or revelations are said to have happened. Others are buildings or monuments believed to contain the relics (sacred remains or possessions) of a holy person. In medieval Christianity, relics of the saints were considered especially powerful and pilgrims flocked to worship them. The city of Canterbury in England became an extremely important pilgrimage site after the murder of Thomas Becket in the cathedral in 1170. Thomas was later made into a saint.

Below: pilgrims visiting St. Thomas Becket's tomb could buy a flask like the one below. It was supposed to contain the saint's diluted blood, thought to have miraculous healing powers.

Above: a painting celebrating the hajj, or pilgrimage to Makkah (Mecca), which all Muslims try to make at least once in their lives. Makkah was the birthplace of the prophet Muhammad.

Right: stupas were originally built to house relics of the Buddha. Later, they represented the quest for enlightenment and became important places of pilgrimage.

Below: Hindu pilgrims bathing in the sacred waters of the River Ganges.

Sacred waters

The holiest places of pilgrimages for Hindus are called *tirthas*, which means crossing places or fords across rivers. These are viewed as crossing places between this world and the next. Most sacred of all is the city of Varanasi on the banks of the holy River Ganges. Bathing in the water of the Ganges is believed to wash sins away. The river is at its most powerful as it flows through Varanasi. Each year, thousands of Hindus visit the city to bathe or to scatter the ashes of loved ones in the river. Most auspicious of all is to die in the city and be cremated on the riverbank.

The Birth of Islam

The word Islam means obedience or submission to Allah (God) and a Muslim is 'someone who surrenders to Allah'. Muslims believe that Allah is the only God, and they accept the message of the prophet Muhammad who founded Islam about 1,400 years ago in the region that is now Saudi Arabia. Muslims believe that Muhammad was the last and greatest in a line of prophets through whom Allah revealed his will and wishes for the world. Islam developed in Makkah (Mecca), Muhammad's birthplace, and later in Madinah (Medina). Today, there are over one billion Muslims in the world, mainly living in the Middle East, Africa and parts of Asia. Islam is the world's second largest religion, after Christianity, and the fastest-growing faith. The worldwide community of Muslims is called the 'Ummah'.

The early prophets
Muslims believe that Allah revealed his message to a series of prophets, beginning with Adam, the first man, (shown on the left with Eve). The prophets included Ibrahim (Abraham), Musa (Moses) and Isa (Jesus), who are also important in Judaism and Christianity.

Below: Musa (Moses), one of the 28 prophets mentioned in the Qur'an.

Right: the birth of Muhammad, shown in a 16th-century Ottoman miniature painting.

The life of Muhammad
The last and greatest prophet, Muhammad, was born in Makkah, in 570 CE. An orphan, he was raised first by his grandfather, then by his uncle. When he was 25, he married a rich widow and worked as a merchant. Although he was rich and successful, Muhammad grew dissatisfied with the way people lived and worshipped. He spent more and more time in quiet contemplation. One night, in 610, as he was meditating on Mount Hira, the angel Jibril appeared and began to reveal Allah's message to him. Many more revelations followed. Muhammad returned to Makkah and began to teach people to worship Allah.

Below: this mythical winged beast called buraq, *or lightning flash, carried Muhammad to Jerusalem on his Night Journey.*

Right: the angel Jibril (Gabriel) revealed Allah's message.

Below: a decorated tile depicting the city of Madinah and the temple area.

The Night Journey
One night, Muhammad is said to have experienced a miraculous event. He was taken by the angel Jibril on a journey from Makkah to Jerusalem. This became known as the Night Journey. There he prayed with the earlier prophets and then travelled up alone through the seven heavens to the throne of Allah himself. Allah told Muhammad that Muslims should pray five times a day.

The flight to Madinah
In Makkah, Muhammad began to teach people that there was one God, Allah, and that they should worship him instead of many idols. Many people started to follow Muhammad but some wealthy Makkans were afraid of his growing popularity, and plotted his death. Eventually, in 622 CE, Muhammad and his followers were forced to leave Makkah. They moved north to Yathrib, later known as Madinah, the City of the Prophet. The journey to Madinah is known as the *Hijrah*, or migration. It is so important that Muslims start their calendar from that date.

SYRIA

• Baghdad

• Jerusalem

Hira •

EGYPT

• Madinah

ARABIA

• Makkah

The spread of Islam by the time of Muhammad's death in 632 CE.

INDIAN OCEAN

Early struggles

In Madinah, the Muslims grew very strong. But they fought many battles with the people of Makkah. The first important battle was at Badr in 624 CE. There the Muslims, though greatly outnumbered, triumphed over the Makkans. In 629, the Muslims conquered Makkah and Muhammad was finally accepted as a great leader.

Below: a sacred image from Iran showing Muslims venerating the Qur'an *and the sandals of Muhammad.*

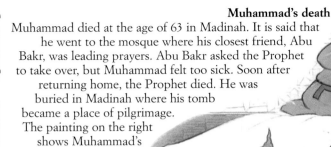

Left: this painting shows Muhammad's followers riding into battle against the Makkans at Badr.

Muhammad's death

Muhammad died at the age of 63 in Madinah. It is said that he went to the mosque where his closest friend, Abu Bakr, was leading prayers. Abu Bakr asked the Prophet to take over, but Muhammad felt too sick. Soon after returning home, the Prophet died. He was buried in Madinah where his tomb became a place of pilgrimage. The painting on the right shows Muhammad's followers weeping at his death.

The Qur'an

The holy book of the Muslims is called the *Qur'an*. It is believed to contain the exact words of Allah, as revealed to Muhammad. Muhammad could not read or write so he recited each verse to his followers, who wrote them down on anything they could find, such as stones or bark. After Muhammad's death, they were collected together in one volume. Muslims believe that the *Qur'an* gives them detailed guidance about how Allah wishes them to live, and they treat it with great respect. They try to read it in the original Arabic, the language in which it was revealed.

Left: a beautifully decorated page from a medieval copy of the Qur'an.

Below: the Abbasids (750–1258 CE) overthrew the Umayyads and made their capital in Baghdad in present-day Iraq. In Egypt, Ibn Tulum fought the Abbasids and constructed the mosque shown here.

Right: a detail from a palace built by the Umayyad rulers. During the Umayyad dynasty (661–750 CE), Islam spread as far west as Spain and as far east as India.

Muslim empires

After Muhammad's death, the Muslims were led by a succession of *caliphs* (khalifas). (The word *caliph* means successor.) The first of these was Muhammad's closest friend, Abu Bakr. Under their leadership, Muslim armies waged many wars outside Arabia, both to defend Islam and also to spread it. These holy wars to defend Islam are known as *jihad*. They also refer to a person's inner struggle against evil or temptation. In just 100 years, Islam had spread across Arabia and into Asia, Europe and North Africa where powerful Muslim empires were established.

Above: in the ninth century Muslims conquered the island of Sicily in the Mediterranean, which became an emirate, or state of a Muslim ruler. Muslim rule in Sicily lasted for about 200 years. Sicily became an important cultural centre of the Muslim world with its castles, mosques and palaces. This ivory horn from Sicily was probably made during Muslim rule.

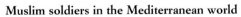

Right: a page from a military handbook written for professional Muslim soldiers in Egypt and Syria.

Muslim soldiers in the Mediterranean world

In the eigth century CE, Muslim armies conquered large parts of Spain and Portugal, and remained in power until the 15th century. In Spain, the Moors (Muslims) created magnificent mosques and palaces, such as the Alhambra in Granada. In another part of the Mediterranean, the mighty Ottoman Empire reached its height in the 16th and 17th centuries. In 1453, Constantinople, the capital of the Christian Byzantine Empire, fell to the Ottoman Turks. The city was renamed Istanbul. The Ottoman Empire ruled Turkey until 1923.

ISLAM

Origins Islam was founded by the prophet Muhammad who was born in 570 CE in modern-day Saudi Arabia.

Beliefs Muslims believe in one God, Allah, who revealed his message to Muhammad. This revelation, known as the Qur'an, is the basis for Muslim life.

Main subdivisions Sunni and Shi'ite.

Adherents over 1 billion.

Sacred texts *Qur'an* and the *Hadiths*.

Muslim Traditions

Muslims all over the world share the same basic set of beliefs. These are called the Five Pillars of Islam because they support the Islamic faith, just as the pillars in a mosque support the building. The Five Pillars are duties given by Allah through the Prophet Muhammad, to be practised in daily life. They teach self-discipline and devotion to Allah. The first is the *Shahadah*, or declaration of faith. It states that, 'There is no God but Allah and Muhammad is the Prophet of Allah.' Muslims believe that Allah created the world and everything in it, and is all-seeing, all-powerful and all-knowing. The second pillar is *Salah*, or prayer. Muslims must pray five times a day between dawn and dusk. The third pillar is *Zakah,* or giving to charity. The fourth pillar is *Sawm*, or fasting during the holy month of Ramadan. The fifth pillar is *Hajj*, making a pilgrimage to the holy city of Makkah.

Above: a silver hand symbolizing the Five Pillars of Islam and the protective hand of Fatima, Muhammad's daughter.

The afterlife

Muslims believe in life after death. They say that two angels stay with people throughout their lives, writing down their good and bad deeds. On the Day of Judgement, Allah will open their book of deeds and make judgement accordingly. Those whose good deeds outweigh their bad deeds will be led by an angel to Paradise. Those whose bad deeds are heavier will fall down into Hell. Only Allah knows when the Day of Judgement will be.

Left: important Muslims were often buried in tombs, where they awaited the Day of Judgement.

Above: Muslims believe that an angel sits on each person's left and right, recording their good and bad deeds.

Pilgrimage to Makkah

The fifth Pillar of Islam is the *Hajj*, or pilgrimage to Makkah which all Muslims try to make at least once in their lives. It takes place each year in the Muslim month of *Dhul Hijjah*. As they enter Makkah, pilgrims change into plain, white clothes to show that they are all equal. They walk seven times around the sacred Ka'aba shrine, then walk or run between two hills, Safa and Marwah. Next they go to Mount Arafat where Muhammad preached his last sermon. At Mina, they throw stones at three pillars which represent the devil.

Left: in celebration of the pilgrimage made to Makkah, Muslims paint images of the Ka'aba, the most sacred Islamic shrine, on their homes.

Above: a Muslim boy praying. Muslims must always face the holy city of Makkah when they pray. They kneel and bow to show their submission to Allah.

Left: a strand of 99 beads used by many Muslims in prayer. Each of the beads stands for one of the names of Allah.

Feast days

Id ul-Adha takes place at the end of the *Hajj*. It remembers how the Prophet Ibrahim was ready to sacrifice his son to obey Allah. A sheep was sacrificed instead. Id ul-Fitr marks the end of Ramadan, the holy month of fasting. It is marked with prayers, parties and giving money to charity.

Right: Ibrahim was ready to sacrifice his son but Allah sent a sheep to take his place.

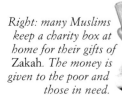

Right: many Muslims keep a charity box at home for their gifts of Zakah. The money is given to the poor and those in need.

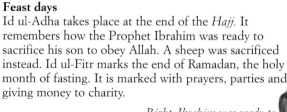

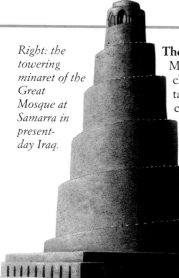

Right: the towering minaret of the Great Mosque at Samarra in present-day Iraq.

The mosque

Muslims can pray to Allah anywhere, as long as they find a clean place or lay a prayer mat on the floor. Many Muslims take part in communal prayers at the *masjid*, or mosque. At certain times during the day, the *muezzin* calls the faithful to prayer from the mosque's tall tower, or minaret. Inside the mosque is a large prayer hall with an arch indicating the direction of Makkah. Men are expected to attend the mosque on Friday for midday prayers. Women sit separately from men. Apart from being a place of worship, the mosque also serves as a community centre and has a school where children learn to read and recite the *Qur'an*.

Left: worshippers must perform a ritual of washing before they enter the mosque to pray.

Below: a Shi'ite standard bearing the names of Allah, Muhammad and Ali.

Below: a Sunni scholar at the Ottoman court in the 16th century.

Below: a Sufi saint, from a 16th-century illustration, is shown listening to the music of a lute player while a fakir sits beside him.

Branches of Islam

After Muhammad's death, two main branches of Islam emerged – the Sunnis and the Shi'ites. About 90 per cent of today's Muslims are Sunni Muslims. They accept the first three *caliphs* as Muhammad's true successors. The Shi'ites do not recognize the first three *caliphs* but see the fourth *caliph*, Ali, as Muhammad's legitimate successor. They believe the leader of Islam must be descended from Ali. Most Shi'ite Muslims live in Iran and Iraq. The Sufis are a group of Muslims who stress a more personal relationship with Allah. Their worship includes music and dancing. For many Sufism meant the abandonment of the material world. Many sufis took a vow of poverty, becoming *fakirs*, or beggars.

Right: a traditional Chinese mosque.

Islam in the world

Islam reached Morocco as early as the seventh century CE. Today, all the countries of North Africa are Muslim. An important part of Islam in present-day Morocco is the veneration of Sufi Muslim saints. There are many festivals throughout the year at which the saints are celebrated with chanting, music and daring horse-riding displays. People also make pilgrimages to the saints' tombs. Islam was brought to China by Muslim traders in the eighth century CE. As in other parts of the Muslim world, the mosque is the central feature of their religious and social life. They call the mosque the 'pure and true' temple.

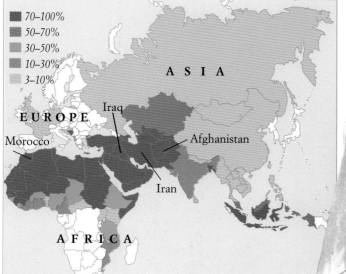

Right: according to the laws of Islam, Muslim men and women should dress modestly, however not all Muslims dress in the same way. These women from Afghanistan are dressed very conservatively, covering their faces.

Map showing percentage of Muslim population in the countries of Asia, Africa and Europe.

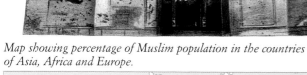

- 70–100%
- 50–70%
- 30–50%
- 10–30%
- 3–10%

ASIA

EUROPE

Iraq

Morocco

Afghanistan

Iran

AFRICA

Islam today

Today, as Islam continues to grow, it faces many challenges. In strongly Muslim countries, the religious laws of Islam, called the *Shari'ah*, are almost the same as the country's laws. In Iran, for example, from 1979–1989 Ayatollah Khomeini led an Islamic revolution and a return to traditional values. He banned all Western influences, bringing Iran into conflict with many other countries. In non-Muslim countries, Muslims are sometimes torn between the desire to follow the *Shari'ah* and also to abide by the laws and customs of the land. For example, for Muslim girls, wearing a school uniform can sometimes conflict with what the *Qur'an* says about clothing.

Left: a drummer leads a procession in Tunisia, North Africa to honour a Muslim saint.

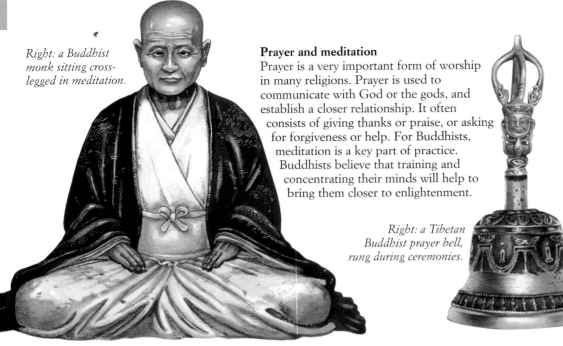

Right: a Buddhist monk sitting cross-legged in meditation.

Prayer and meditation

Prayer is a very important form of worship in many religions. Prayer is used to communicate with God or the gods, and establish a closer relationship. It often consists of giving thanks or praise, or asking for forgiveness or help. For Buddhists, meditation is a key part of practice. Buddhists believe that training and concentrating their minds will help to bring them closer to enlightenment.

Right: a Tibetan Buddhist prayer bell, rung during ceremonies.

Below: many daily activities of Jewish life involve rituals and prayer. This Jewish man is preparing for morning prayers. He is wearing a tallit *robe and two* tefillin *black leather boxes containing parchment scrolls with passages from the* Torah. *One of them is placed on the head and the other on the arm pointing to the heart. The* tefillin *remind the wearer to dedicate himself both with his mind and heart to God.*

Forms of Worship

Whatever their differences, all religions share some form of worship or prayer. In many religions, followers visit a place of worship, such as a mosque or church, to praise God and say their prayers. Others have different ways of communicating with God or the gods, through offerings, dance and songs of praise. Prayer may be part of a set service, or of group worship, which may also include listening to talks or reading passages from the sacred texts. But for many people, prayer is a personal, private act to be performed quietly at home. In most religions, special ceremonies are held to celebrate key events in the religion's history and in worshippers' lives. Each ceremony has its own set of rites and rituals, often with very ancient origins. These occasions are a chance for members of a faith to join together in their happiness or grief. Rites and rituals help people cope with difficult times in their lives, like when a loved one dies, and share happy times.

Left: a mask from Oceania, worn during an initiation rite when boys entered adulthood.

Left: some of the objects used in a Zoroastrian ceremony of thanksgiving.

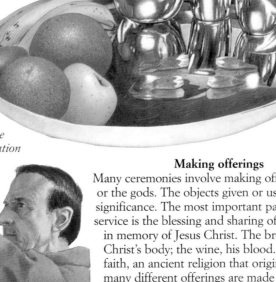

Below: a figure of a worshipper paying homage to the goddess Kuan Yin (see page 28) with burning incense, from a 10th-century Chinese painting.

Rites of passage

In most of the world's faiths, the important times in a person's life, such as birth, adulthood, marriage and death, are marked with special ceremonies. These rites of passage are like signposts on the journey through life, guiding people through the different stages. Each rite has its own set customs, like special prayers, festive food and clothes and the exchange of gifts. The object on the left is a snuff spoon. Among some African peoples, it is a sign of adulthood when a boy takes snuff.

Below: a Roman Catholic priest blessing the wine during a celebration of Mass.

Making offerings

Many ceremonies involve making offerings to God or the gods. The objects given or used have special significance. The most important part of a Christian service is the blessing and sharing of bread and wine in memory of Jesus Christ. The bread represents Christ's body; the wine, his blood. In the Zoroastrian faith, an ancient religion that originated in Persia, many different offerings are made during a ceremony of thanksgiving. The Zoroastrians, followers of the teachings of the prophet Zoroaster (Zarathrustra), perform the thanksgiving ceremony to maintain the balance of the world. The objects symbolize the seven bounteous immortals – sky, water, earth, plants, cattle, people and fire – on which the well-being of the world depends.

Right: for the members of the Kamiura tribe of Brazil, the music of their flutes is considered to be the voice of the spirits.

Above: a group of Sufi dancers, known as whirling dervishes.

Right: this Confucian musician's music accompanies ritual ceremonies in South Korea.

Music and dance

According to some legends and traditions, music is a gift of the gods. The ancient Greeks worshipped Apollo, god of music, who is often depicted holding his lyre (see page 10). Today, music and dance are often fundamental parts of rituals. Some religions use music and dance as a way of feeling closer or communicating with God or the gods. Music can be a way for many to express joy or sorrow. One group of Muslims, the Sufis perform spectacular ritual dances, spinning faster and faster to the sound of pipes and tambourines to praise their god.

Left: in the traditional religion of Hawaii, drums are beaten to summon worshippers to the temple and as part of temple rites and rituals.

Appeasing God

In some religions, ceremonies were performed to gain approval from God or the gods. For centuries, appeasing the gods was considered crucial in averting disaster, such as drought or poor harvest. In the Middle Ages, the Black Death that swept across Europe, killing millions of people, was seen as a punishment from God for people's sins. Groups of hooded men, right, wearing white robes marked with a red cross, showed their remorse by beating themselves with whips studded with iron spikes.

Consulting the gods

For thousands of years, people have looked to omens, oracles and natural signs to discover the will of the gods. For example, in ancient Greece and Rome, no one would dare to embark on a journey without asking the gods for their blessing first. The picture above shows a group of Confucian diviners consulting the *I Ching* (Book of Changes), a key Confucian text. The man on the right throws his bundle of sticks on the floor. Then the pattern of lines is matched to those in the *I Ching* to predict the future.

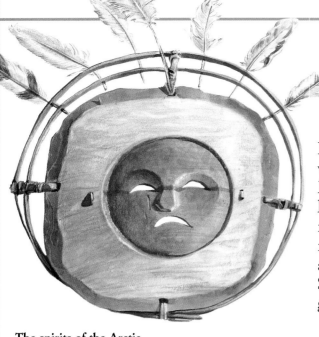

Spirit Religions of the Americas

From the Arctic regions in the north, to Patagonia in the south, a wide variety of traditional religious beliefs are practised in the Americas. Many of these are based on the worship of spirits that are believed to live in animals, trees and natural places. They reflect people's relationship with nature which is seen as a force to be both feared and revered. Nature also played an important part in the religions of the ancient Aztec and Inca civilizations which flourished in Central and South America. It was essential to keep the gods happy to ensure a good harvest and keep order in the world.

The spirits of the Arctic

Traditionally, the Inuit people of the Arctic were able to survive in their harsh world by hunting animals, such as seals, walruses and whales. The Inuit believe that every animal has a spirit which must be respected. When an animal is killed, the hunter performs a ceremony to make sure that its spirit returns to be hunted again. Another important Inuit spirit is the Moon Spirit, above, a mighty hunter, who controls the animals from his home in the sky.

Shamanism

In many traditional societies, shamans play an important role as messengers between the human and spirit world. In times of famine, Inuit shamans are believed to have the power to visit the spirit world in the sea to ask Sedna, the sea goddess, to release seals for hunting.

Below: an Inuit shaman's charm, carved from ivory.

Right: an evil spirit from Greenland.

Spirit carving

Like the Inuit, the Native Americans of North America believe that every living thing has a spirit, good or bad. Many of the spirits take the form of animals which people carve on masks or totem poles. Masks, like the one of a grizzly bear shown below, are worn at feasts and ceremonies to act out the exploits of the spirits. The carved images on a totem pole represent a clan's founding spirits and the spirits that guard and protect it.

Good and evil

The peoples of the Woodlands, like many other Native Americans, believe in the ongoing struggle between good and evil spirits. The evil spirits are destructive and cause human illness and disease. In order to keep these spirits away, and to prevent illness, the Native Americans perform special ceremonies. Masks, like the one on the left, are worn during ceremonies in which offerings are made to the spirits. The face of the mask, intended to represent a spirit of nature, has bulging eyes and a terrifying smile to scare away the evil spirits.

NORTH AMERICA

Mississippi River

Arctic region
Northern forests
West and north-west
Plains
South-west
Woodlands and south-east

Map showing the traditional cultural areas of the Native Americans.

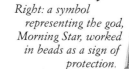

Left: a Hopi kachina *doll of Masau'u, the Earth god, who rules the earth and oversees the journey of the dead from the Earth to the Underworld.*

Right: a grizzly bear mask worn in ritual dances from the north-west coast.

The first beings

Native Americans have many myths which tell how the world began. The Hopi people of the south-west believe that there were once four worlds – this world and three cave worlds beneath it. The first creatures lived in the bottom cave but, when that grew dirty and overcrowded, they climbed up a plant to the caves above until they finally reached this world.

Right: a symbol representing the god, Morning Star, worked in beads as a sign of protection.

The Great Spirit

Many Native Americans share the belief in a supreme being, called the Great Spirit, who created the world. The lesser gods and spirits act as messengers between the Great Spirit and the Earth. One of the most important gods is Morning Star, to whom the Great Spirit entrusted the gift of life to spread over the Earth.

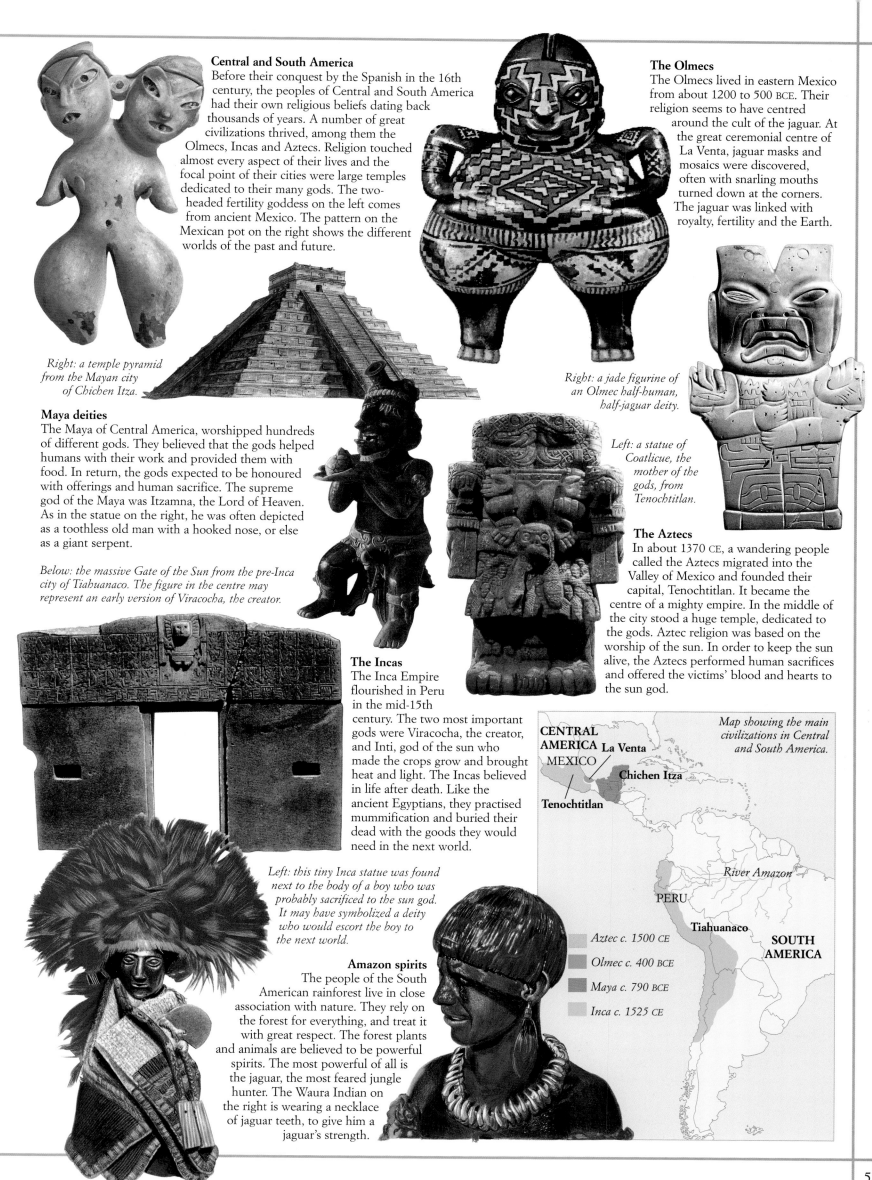

Central and South America

Before their conquest by the Spanish in the 16th century, the peoples of Central and South America had their own religious beliefs dating back thousands of years. A number of great civilizations thrived, among them the Olmecs, Incas and Aztecs. Religion touched almost every aspect of their lives and the focal point of their cities were large temples dedicated to their many gods. The two-headed fertility goddess on the left comes from ancient Mexico. The pattern on the Mexican pot on the right shows the different worlds of the past and future.

The Olmecs

The Olmecs lived in eastern Mexico from about 1200 to 500 BCE. Their religion seems to have centred around the cult of the jaguar. At the great ceremonial centre of La Venta, jaguar masks and mosaics were discovered, often with snarling mouths turned down at the corners. The jaguar was linked with royalty, fertility and the Earth.

Right: a temple pyramid from the Mayan city of Chichen Itza.

Right: a jade figurine of an Olmec half-human, half-jaguar deity.

Maya deities

The Maya of Central America, worshipped hundreds of different gods. They believed that the gods helped humans with their work and provided them with food. In return, the gods expected to be honoured with offerings and human sacrifice. The supreme god of the Maya was Itzamna, the Lord of Heaven. As in the statue on the right, he was often depicted as a toothless old man with a hooked nose, or else as a giant serpent.

Below: the massive Gate of the Sun from the pre-Inca city of Tiahuanaco. The figure in the centre may represent an early version of Viracocha, the creator.

Left: a statue of Coatlicue, the mother of the gods, from Tenochtitlan.

The Aztecs

In about 1370 CE, a wandering people called the Aztecs migrated into the Valley of Mexico and founded their capital, Tenochtitlan. It became the centre of a mighty empire. In the middle of the city stood a huge temple, dedicated to the gods. Aztec religion was based on the worship of the sun. In order to keep the sun alive, the Aztecs performed human sacrifices and offered the victims' blood and hearts to the sun god.

The Incas

The Inca Empire flourished in Peru in the mid-15th century. The two most important gods were Viracocha, the creator, and Inti, god of the sun who made the crops grow and brought heat and light. The Incas believed in life after death. Like the ancient Egyptians, they practised mummification and buried their dead with the goods they would need in the next world.

Left: this tiny Inca statue was found next to the body of a boy who was probably sacrificed to the sun god. It may have symbolized a deity who would escort the boy to the next world.

Map showing the main civilizations in Central and South America.

CENTRAL AMERICA
La Venta
MEXICO
Chichen Itza
Tenochtitlan

River Amazon

PERU

Tiahuanaco

SOUTH AMERICA

Aztec c. 1500 CE
Olmec c. 400 BCE
Maya c. 790 BCE
Inca c. 1525 CE

Amazon spirits

The people of the South American rainforest live in close association with nature. They rely on the forest for everything, and treat it with great respect. The forest plants and animals are believed to be powerful spirits. The most powerful of all is the jaguar, the most feared jungle hunter. The Waura Indian on the right is wearing a necklace of jaguar teeth, to give him a jaguar's strength.

Below: a wooden dish representing the 'ark' in which Nommo and the other gods came down to Earth.

Creation myths

In traditional African religions, many stories are told about how the world came to be. Most tell of a great spirit who created the world. The Dogon people of Mali believe that creation began with a being called Amma, an egg that was the seed of the universe. It burst open to reveal Nommo, father of mankind, who fell to Earth with several other gods. They created the sky, the Earth, day and night, the seasons and human beings, and put them into order. The Fon people of Nigeria believe that the world was created by the moon and the sun, and is held together by a sacred snake.

Below: a Fon bowl from Nigeria showing a man and woman with the sacred python wrapped around the world.

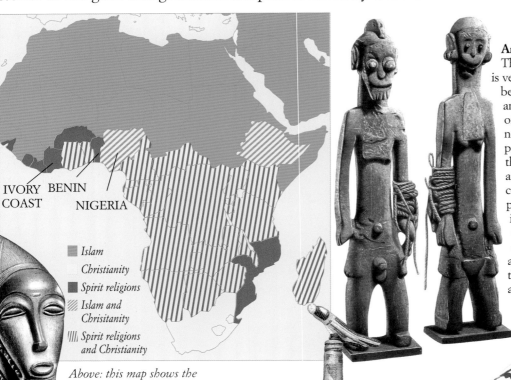

Spirit Religions of Africa and Oceania

Although mainstream religions, including Christianity and Islam, are now widely practised in many parts of Africa and Oceania, traditional beliefs still survive in many communities. Like those of the Americas, these beliefs reflect people's close relationship with the natural world around them, on which they depend for shelter and food. If they are treated with proper respect, the spirits are thought to reward their followers with good harvests or hunting. Elaborate rituals and ceremonies are held to worship them, and, in societies with no tradition of writing, stories of the gods and goddesses are passed down by word of mouth.

IVORY COAST BENIN NIGERIA

- ■ Islam
- Christianity
- ■ Spirit religions
- ⧄ Islam and Christianity
- ⦀ Spirit religions and Christianity

Above: this map shows the religions practised by the majority in African countries.

Ancestor worship

The worship of ancestors is very important in African belief. The spirits of the ancestors must be revered in order to live peacefully in the next world. In return, they protect the living and guard their homes. The two ancestor figures on the left come from Nigeria. They are paraded through the village in times of danger and during funerals and other ceremonies, when they act as a link between the priest and the ancestors' world.

Right: a charm belonging to an African healer, probably used in rituals in which the ancestors' power is invoked.

Right: a royal calabash (gourd) used as a musical instrument or to hold an ancestor's bones at a religious ritual.

Spirit carvings

The wooden statue on the left comes from the Ivory Coast. It was carved to incarnate (give a body to) a bush spirit called Asie Usu. A mischievous spirit, Asie Usu will, if properly worshipped, grant fruitful harvests and hunts. Statues like these are made for people's homes where they are honoured with offerings of eggs and chicken blood.

Art and ritual

In the Fon kingdoms of Western Africa, art is created to help people contact the spirits and to give homage to the king. After a divination ceremony, in which a special name for the king is given, artists create visual representations of this name. Other objects named during the divination ceremony are made by specialist craftspeople. These include metal ornaments, wood carvings and textiles decorated with special designs used for banners, umbrellas and canopies.

Right: a Fon king of Dahomey in Benin wearing a silver nose cover to help him to communicate with his ancestors.

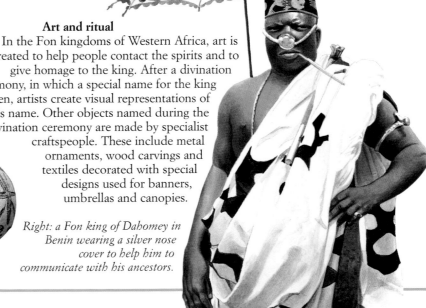

The Dreamtime

The Aborigine people of Australia believe that the world was made long ago, in a time called the Dreamtime. This was the time when the ancestors travelled across Australia, shaping society and the landscape which had been dark, flat and featureless. Then some rose into the sky and became stars, while others turned into rocks, trees, waterholes, birds and animals, still visible today. For Aborigines, the land is sacred and must be looked after. Special rituals are held to remember the Dreamtime when dancers briefly become the ancestors and recreate their ancient journeys.

Above: an Aborigine bark painting illustrating a creation myth.

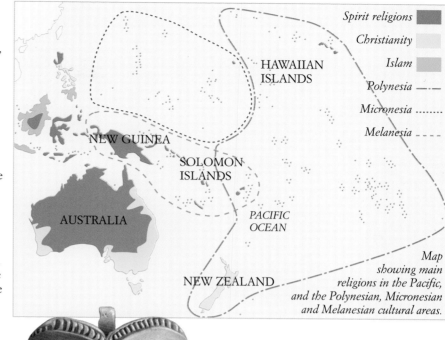

Map showing main religions in the Pacific, and the Polynesian, Micronesian and Melanesian cultural areas.

Spirit religions
Christianity
Islam
Polynesia — —
Micronesia ....
Melanesia – – –

Right: a carved wooden mask of a mythological figure from New Zealand. According to Maori tradition, the god Rua made the first carvings.

Left: a Maori hei-tiki pendant. The Maori believe that Tiki was the name of the first man. He married Hina, the first woman. She was patron of women's crafts and guardian of the dead.

Above: wooden figures of the ancestral being Djanggawul with his two sisters. They arrived from the sea and taught people how to dig waterholes and grow crops.

Polynesian gods

Polynesia stretches from New Zealand in the south to Hawaii in the north. Among the most important gods of the Maori of New Zealand are Rangi, the sky god, and Papa, goddess of the Earth. Their children were the gods of the forests, crops, the sea, plants and the winds. Legends also tell of many heroes and lesser gods, including the mischievous Maui. He is said to have pulled the islands of New Zealand out of the sea, having mistaken them for a giant fish.

Right: a Hawaiian sculpture of Kukailimoku, or Ku, god of the Earth and war.

Beliefs of Melanesia

Papua New Guinea and the islands of the south-west Pacific form the region called Melanesia. The islands share many of the same beliefs but also have their own particular spirits and rituals. The sea plays a vital role in their lives. They believe that it was released by the first beings who came down from heaven. Many of the gods they worship are spirits of the sea or of fishing.

Right: an ornament from the Solomon Islands used to decorate the prow of a canoe. It shows a god of fishing.

The House of the Spirits

In Papua New Guinea, some houses, like the one shown on the right, are built to commemorate village ancestors. This building is called a House of the Spirits and was built by the Abelam people. During initiation ceremonies and harvest festivals, the inside of the house is decorated with wood carvings and paintings of the ancestors. The house lies in the centre of a ritual ground reserved for men. During the ceremonies images of the ancestors are shown to the the initiates. At the end of the rituals, the boys paint their bodies and begin a procession from the house.

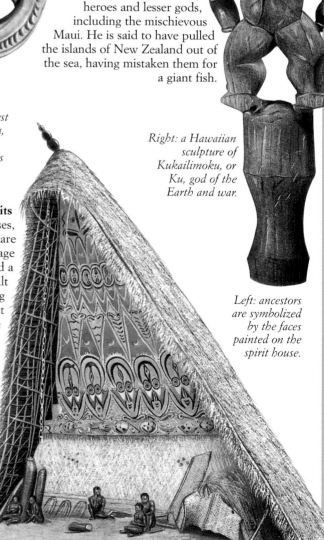

Left: ancestors are symbolized by the faces painted on the spirit house.

Religious revival

Many new religious movements are based on established, mainstream faiths, such as Christianity, Islam and Hinduism. While some of these movements have gained many followers, some have met opposition. One of the best-known Hindu-inspired groups is the International Society for Krishna Consciousness (ISKON, also called the Hare Krishna Movement). Founded in 1966 by a Hindu holy man, Bhaktivedanta Swami Prabhupada, devotees worship the god Krishna and chant a *mantra* (short prayer) based on his name. The movement has grown worldwide. Thousands have been attracted by its teachings of giving up attachment to material things and concentrating on inner peace instead.

Right: the Unification Church, or 'Moonies', a new religion based on Christian ideas, was founded by the Reverend Sun Myung Moon in 1954. Some people have criticized its controversial teachings.

Left: Hare Krishna devotees chant, dance and play drums and cymbals as they parade through the streets.

New Religions and Religious Movements

Throughout history, new religious movements have emerged as people continue to debate the answers to some of life's oldest and trickiest questions. Some of these new groups have developed within long-established religions, offering new interpretations of old beliefs. Other groups have broken away completely to become independent religions in their own right. Dissatisfaction with existing religions can lead to the founding of entirely new groups, with new leaders, rituals and beliefs.

Religion and local traditions

In some places, mainstream religion mixes with local beliefs. Voodoo is the main folk religion of Haiti. It is a mixture of Roman Catholic beliefs and African religious and magical traditions. Followers of voodoo believe in spirits called *loa* who represent ancestors, African deities and Christian saints. To communicate with the *loa*, they hold services which involve singing, dancing, beating drums, prayers and animal sacrifices.

Below: the Rastafarian tradition of growing hair in dreadlocks and growing beards derives from a passage found in the Bible.

Christian movements

Many new religious movements have grown out of Christianity. Some are based on different interpretations of the Bible. Others were inspired by divine revelations and visions. The Church of the Latter Day Saints, or Mormons, bases its beliefs on the *Book of Mormon*. It is said to have been revealed to the Mormon founder, Joseph Smith (1805–1844), in 1822. The headquarters of the Mormon Church is in Salt Lake City, Utah. Mormons believe that Jesus visited America and will come again to defeat the forces of evil. Mormons lead a strict life and do not smoke or drink alcohol, tea or coffee. Hard work and a good education are highly valued.

Above: the angel revealing the Book of Mormon *to founder, Joseph Smith.*

Televised religion

Although the number of people attending church has declined in the last few decades, Christian evangelist preachers are reaching wider audiences than ever before. These 'tele-evangelists' use television and rock-style concerts to spread their message to millions of people all over the world.

Right: tele-evangelist, Jimmy Swaggart.

Return to freedom

Rastafarianism was founded in Jamaica in the 1930s. Ras ('Prince') Tafari, Emperor Haile Selassie of Ethiopia (1892–1975), was hailed as the new black messiah. Rastafarian beliefs are a mixture of biblical teachings and African beliefs. One day, they believe, they will return to freedom in Africa from exile in the countries to which their ancestors were taken as slaves.

Rigth: new teaching and meditation centres have sprung up in the West. The emblem of the Buddhist Madaron Shambhasalem monastery in the French Alps reads, 'I am in you, you are in me. We are as one.'

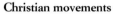

JE SUIS EN TOI, TU ES EN MOI. NOUS SOMMES dans l'UN

Religion in the West

New branches of Islam and Buddhism have developed in the West. Although they are based on the same fundamental teachings, these movements have provided new interpretations and ways of worshipping. The Nation of Islam, founded in the United States in the 1930s, is a controversial branch of Islam. Its followers, called Black Muslims, seek social justice and equality for black people, based on the teachings of the *Qur'an* and the Bible.

Right: members of the Nation of Islam sign their names with an X instead of using the family names given to their ancestors by their slave owners. Malcolm X (Malcolm Little) was a spokesman for the group.

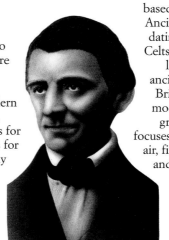

Left: Greek mathematician and philosopher Pythagoras (c. 580–500 BCE) and his followers based their religious beliefs on numbers.

Philosophy and religion

Religion and philosophy are closely linked. Both try to find the answers to the mysteries of life. However, they are also very different. One looks for the answers in the existence of God; the other in the pursuit of knowledge. Modern philosophy of religion is a subject which combines the two. It looks at the reasons for religious belief, especially the arguments for God's existence. The religious philosophy known as theosophy (a term formed by the combination of the Greek words for god and wisdom), with roots in ancient Greek philosophy, has had a great impact on modern thinkers. Ralph Waldo Emerson gave up his ministry in the Unitarian Church to teach a philosophy called Transcendentalism. He urged people to trust their own instincts and to find the divine in themselves.

Above: Ralph Waldo Emerson (1803–1882).

Ancient traditions

Some new religious movements are based on ancient spiritual beliefs. Ancient Druidism is a tradition dating back to the time of the Celts (see pages 12–13). In the last century, interest in the ancient Druids has revived in Britain and many groups of modern-day Druids have grown. Their worship focuses on the elements of air, fire, water and earth, and centres on ancient sacred sites, such as the stone circles at Stonehenge and Avebury.

Right: a modern-day Druid arriving at Stonehenge to perform sacred rites at midsummer.

Below: a tarot card showing the sun. Some people consult tarot cards to foresee the future. The sun symbolizes hope, light and life.

New Age movements

The term 'New Age' is used to describe a wide range of groups, all loosely connected. New Age movements range from astrology and the green movement, to alternative medicine and occultism, mixed with some traditions from Eastern religion. Followers believe that the world is entering a 'new age' of spirituality. They focus on the healing of the body, mind and spirit to channel the Earth's unseen energy forces and bring about a sense of health and well-being.

New religions facing persecution

Not all new religions are openly accepted. Some founders of new religions faced strong persecution. Siyyid Ali-Muhammad, a Shi'a Muslim claimed to be a new prophet calling himself the *Bab*, or 'gate' to God. Accused of heresy, he was executed in 1850 and his followers were arrested. Before his death he announced the coming of another prophet. After the *Bab's* death the prophet Baha'u'llah revealed himself and founded the Baha'i religion in modern day Iran. He taught that all religions should unite and that people should strive to bring peace to the world. Baha'u'llah, exiled in modern day Israel, spread his message through his writings which were later interpreted by his son, Abdu'l-Baha who spread Baha'ism worldwide.

Right: some who practise occultism, using astrology and magic, are called 'witches'. Many of these practices are not approved by mainstream religions.

Below: this symbol represents the Falun Gong movement which spread throughout China after 1992. Followers practise with simple exercises and meditation to attain a healthy and peaceful way of life. The movement has been brutally repressed by the Chinese government.

Above: the shrine of the Bab on Mount Carmel in Israel.

New state religions

Developments in religion and political movements have influenced each other. In Vietnam, the Cao Dai sect, founded in 1926, had a strong impact on national politics. In other areas, such as North Korea where traditional religions such as Buddhism and Christianity have been condemned by the government, a new religion, called Juche, has developed. Kim Jong Il, the 'Dear Leader', and his father, Kim Il-Sung, the 'Great Leader', are worshipped as the divine progenitors and protectors of the people. Worshippers keep images of their heroic leaders in their homes and leave wreaths at Kim Il-Sung's memorial in Pyongyan to honour him and mourn his death.

Left: the Cao Dai symbol of the eye represents the Supreme Being. Cao Daiists follow the teachings of Buddhism, Taoism, Confucianism and Christianity and they believe that all religions express the same truth.

Sharing beliefs

Many religions have beliefs in common, although their interpretations may vary considerably. Islam, for example, believes in Abraham, Moses and Jesus as great prophets. Prophets are also important for Jews and Christians. In China, the religions they founded have existed for centuries side by side. The picture on the left shows three great religious teachers – Lao Tzu, the Buddha and Confucius.

Left: this picture shows Moses with the prophet Muhammad.

Left: a 19th-century sword guard with the figures of Lao Tzu, the Buddha and Confucius.

Tolerance and Intolerance

Many of the world's religions share certain beliefs and practices in common. Most provide their followers with a moral code for living and try to give answers to difficult questions to explain, for example, how the world began and what happens after death. Throughout history, however, it is the differences between religions which have made the news. When these conflicts arise in countries already facing difficulties, such as political power struggles or economic problems, they can quickly lead to the persecution of religious minorities, and even to war. Religion also faces the challenge of reconciling its traditional beliefs with the demands of the modern world. Many people hope that the future lies in greater tolerance and understanding between the different faiths. Indeed, many see this as the only way that religion around the world can face up to the future.

Below: a Christian Crusader knight with the typical cross insignia.

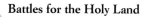

Left: during the Middle Ages texts which expressed the ideas of heretics were destroyed.

Left: the Roman emperor Nero is notorious for his cruelty towards the early Christians in ancient Rome.

Battles for the Holy Land

Over the centuries, religious leaders and rulers have sometimes encouraged people to go to war to defend their religious beliefs. Between the end of the 11th and 13th centuries, Christian armies from Europe went on a series of military pilgrimages, or Crusades, to the Holy Land. They were called to arms from Rome by Pope Urban II. Their aim was to capture Jerusalem from the Muslim Turks who sought to defend their faith and carry out God's will (see page 45). The Muslims, whose duty it is to defend and spread Islam, made many *jihads*, or holy wars. The Crusades inspired many stories of great bravery and honour in the name of religion. But they also had a less noble side, with cases of cruelty and violence.

Above: the Spanish burn an Aztec courtier.

Religious persecution

Throughout history, heretics, or people who go against mainstream beliefs or official religion, have suffered persecution. In the Middle Ages, many small, scattered groups of Jews lived throughout Europe, in mainly Christian countries. They were persecuted for their beliefs and were forced to leave their homes. In the early 16th century, the Aztecs of Mexico were conquered by the Spanish who claimed their lands for God and the king. Thousands of Aztecs were killed.

Below: these Muslims from Uzbekistan, formerly part of the Soviet Union, pray at a local mosque.

Free to worship

In many parts of the world religious groups are not free to worship as they please. Many have been suppressed by governments or by other religious groups. Many groups have emigrated to other parts of the world in search of religious freedom. In recent years, following the fall of the Soviet Union, many more worshippers now enjoy religious freedom.

Left: in the 18th century a Christian reform group known as the Amish emigrated to North America in search of religious freedom . This manuscript of a Biblical psalm was made by a group of these early immigrants.

Victims of the state

The persecution of the Jews reached its worst excess during World War II (1939–1945). Six million Jews were brutally killed by the German Nazis. This is known as the Holocaust. Many were gassed to death in concentration camps while many others died from disease or starvation. In Russia, the Revolution of 1917 had raised the Russian Jews' hopes that they would be treated as equal citizens. But they continued to suffer. Joseph Stalin, left, came to power in 1924. Under his oppressive rule, thousands of Jews were arrested, deported and killed. By the time of the German invasion in 1941, the destruction of Jewish life had already begun.

Above: the gates of Auschwitz, a Nazi concentration camp.

Right: Joseph Stalin (1879–1953).

Below: a Pueblo Indian chief from New Mexico, USA.

Living together

In the 20th century, many people from the developing world have emigrated to wealthier, industrialized countries in search of a better life. They have brought their religious beliefs and customs with them. In many places this has enriched the culture of their new homelands. In other places emigration has threatened the culture of native people. Many communities are now fighting to preserve them. For example, the remains of thousands of Native American ancestors in New Mexico, removed from their graves 80 years ago, have recently been returned to their families and reburied according to their sacred rites.

Dealing with diversity

After years of bitter fighting between Muslims and Hindus, India was divided. In 1947 Pakistan and East Pakistan (now Bangladesh) were formed. Millions of people moved in or out of India according to their religion. Today Pakistan has become an Islamic state while the majority of people in India are Hindu. The violence still continues. In India leaders must deal with frequent violent outbreaks between Muslims and Hindus.

Below: in 1992 Hindu extremists destroyed a mosque in Uttar Pradesh, India, claiming that it stood on a Hindu site.

Left: this ancient statue of the Buddha is now gone for ever.

Destruction of sacred images

In March 2001, two ancient statues of the Buddha in Afghanistan were deliberately blown up by the ruling Muslim Taliban regime. The huge statues had stood for almost 2,000 years, carved out of the cliff face. Despite requests from the United Nations and neighbouring governments that the statues be saved, or even removed from the area, the Taliban decreed that the statues were evidence of idol worship (which is not permitted in the Islamic faith) and destroyed them in the name of religion.

Quest for peace

Since the formation of the State of Israel in 1948, in what was formerly Palestine, there has been constant conflict between Israel's Jewish population and the Palestinian Arabs who are mainly Muslim and Christian. Civil wars and political upheaval have made the area very unstable. Both the United Nations and the United States have tried to bring about understanding but progress has been slow. In 1993 political leaders met for peace talks and to discuss Palestinian self-rule. However, in 2000-02, the violence between the two sides increased greatly.

Above: US President Bill Clinton, centre, brought together the Palestinian leader, Yasser Arafat, and the Israeli prime minister, Yitzhak Rabin.

A mission of forgiveness

In 2001 Pope John Paul II, leader of the Roman Catholic Church, made a historic pilgrimage to Syria where he became the first pope to enter a mosque. Following Muslim practice, the Pope took off his shoes before entering the Great Omayyad mosque, one of the most important places of worship for Muslims. The Pope was received by Muslim leaders, including the Grand Mufti of Syria. The purpose of his pilgrimage was to ask Muslims and Christians all over the world to forgive each other for all of the violence of the past. He stated that religious beliefs are never a just cause for war and violence.

Left: Pope John Paul II became Pope in 1978.

Bottom: a map of religious freedom in the year 2000.

In FREE countries citizens enjoy a high degree of religious freedom.

PARTLY FREE countries are characterized by some restrictions on religious freedom, often in a context of corruption, weak rule of law, ethnic strife or civil war.

In NOT FREE countries, religion is tightly controlled and basic religious freedom is denied.

This map was reproduced by courtesy of Freedom House

www.freedomhouse.org

- Free
- Partly free
- Not free

Index